D1505287

Great Central
Memories

Great Central Memories

JOHN HEALY

Baton Transport

Dedication

To my parents who have put up with me while working on the book and helped wherever possible, my girlfriend Julie and everyone who has been involved with the Great Central both past and present.

Other Baton Transport Titles:

Scottish Steam Routes
The Settle to Carlisle
The Welsh Marches
Roger Siviter

Midland Line Memories
Midland through the Peak
Brian Radford

The Final Link
Metro-Memories
The Romance of Metroland
The Golden Years of the Metropolitan Railway
London's Underground Suburbs
Dennis Edwards and Ron Pigram

London's Underground Stations
Laurence Menear

Down the Line to Brighton
Down the Line to Bristol
Down the Line to Dover
Down the Line to Southend
Muriel V. Searle

Down the Line to Hastings
Brian Jewell

First Published in 1987 by
BATON TRANSPORT
1 Russell Chambers
Covent Garden
London, WC2E 8AA

© John M. C. Healy

ISBN 0 85936 193 4

All rights reserved. No part of this publication may be reproduced, stored in a retrieval system, or transmitted in any form or by any means, electronic, mechanical, photocopying, recorded or otherwise, without the prior permission of the publisher.

Design by Words and Images
Typeset by Vitaset, Paddock Wood, Kent
Printed and bound by Robert Hartnoll (1985) Ltd, Bodmin, Cornwall.

The Author

John Healy has been fascinated with railways from his early childhood when he had the opportunity to ride behind one of the last steam trains from Euston to Manchester. Educated at Berkhamsted School, Hertfordshire, which was conveniently placed next to the busiest part of the West Coast Main Line, he managed to pursue his interests in the railway field but with particular emphasis on the historical and social impact of the Great Central on society, paving the way for the writing of this book. Now an Undergraduate student of Classics at University College, London, he has become involved at weekends with the Great Central Railway at Loughborough where he holds the honorary post of Museum Curator.

He has published a number of articles in Railway Journals and, having carried out a long and detailed research into the life of Sydney Newton (the London Extension Photographer), he compiled a book published by Leicester Museums services, called the *Great Central Through the Eyes of S.W.A. Newton* using the 'Then and Now' theme with the addition of some of his own pictures.

Among his other interests he enjoys local history, travel, music and photography and is a member of the Woodford Halse Great Central Railway Enthusiasts Association. The club is dedicated to reliving the glorious years of steam and has a spectacular model layout of old Woodford Halse in its former years and offers slide shows the second Wednesday of every month.

Contents

Acknowledgements

The author wishes to express his gratitude to the countless friends, former Great Central employees and numerous organisations who have all so willingly given help and advice in the preparation of this work. I would also like to thank the many enthusiastic photographers who have generously provided me with a wealth of illustrations – many previously unpublished. Special thanks are due to Mr. G.A. Chinnery, the Deputy Director of Leicester Museums, for help on many occasions, to the late Mr. R. Pigram for his constructive advice from which I have greatly benefited, Mr. Ron Alder of Little Chalfont for reading the proofs and finally, to Mr. Vic Forster who was responsible for bringing a number of important sources to my attention.

In addition to my own research I have consulted, among other works, the following: George Dow: *Great Central Album*; Colin Walker: *Main Line Lament*; C.R.L. Coles: *Railways through the Chilterns*; and M. Davis and R. Grant: *Forgotten Railways in the Chilterns and Cotswolds*.

I would also like to place on record my thanks to John Murray Ltd for permission to quote the late Sir John Betjeman's evocative poem 'Sheffield Victoria to Banbury'.

Credits

The author gratefully acknowledges the following individuals and organizations who have willingly supplied illustrations for this book. Without their help the various subjects could not have been so well covered. The numbers quoted refer to page numbers, and the position on the page is indicated thus: T = Top, C = Centre, B =Bottom.

British Railways: 42(B) 43(B).
J. Clarke: 66(C).
C. R. L. Coles: 51.
Colour Rail: 73(B), 74(B), 136(B), 142, 143(T).
J. G. Coltas: courtesy of R. Wallis 50(C), 52, 83, 100(B), 101, 109(T), 121, 122.
K. C. H. Fairey: 66(T), 88(B), 89(T), 91(T) & (C), 97(T), 98(C), 102, 103, 117(B), 124, 125(T), 126–129, 132(T), 134, 135(T) & (B), 143(B), 146(B), 160.
V. Forster: 66(B), 67(T) & (C), 68(B), 69(B), 71(C), 75(T), 99(C), 150(B), 151(T).
Great Central Railway Museum, Loughborough: 9, 12, 14, 22(B), 25(B), 44, 56, 57, 59, 62, 75(B), 77, 78, 79(B), 80, 82, 97(B), 105, 123, 133, 157(B).
L. Hanson: 94(C), 95, 97(T).
J. F. Henton: 58(B), 64(T), 67(B), 69(T) & (C), 70(B), 71(T), 73(C), 85(T), 86(T), 144, 145, 146(T).

Leicester Museums: 13, 15, 16, 18–21, 22(T), 23, 24, 25(T), 26–42(T), 45, 46(B), 47–50(T) & (B), 53(C) & (B), 84, 87, 88(T), 88/89, 90, 106, 109(B), 112, 113, 119(C), 120.
M. Marston: 93(B), 94(B).
J. B. McCann: 96, 98(T).
National Railway Museum, York: 11.
Northampton Library: 114(B), 166.
Nottingham City Council: 70(T), 72, 73(T), 74(T) & (C).
Oxford City Library 118, 132(B).
Real Photographs: 43(T), 46(T), 53(T), 54, 58(T), 71(B), 75(C), 76(B), 79(C), 81, 85(C), 86(B), 93(C), 94(T), 99(B), 100(T) & (C), 104, 107, 108, 114(T), 115(T), 119(T).
E. G. Shoults, courtesy J. Clarke: 91(B), 92.
Ron White, 55, 64(C) & (B), 65, 135(C), 136(T), 137–141.
Other photographs are from the author's collection.

Preface

The Great Central Railway, the last main line route into London, which covered the 135 miles between Annesley and Marylebone, finally closed in 1966 after a chequered history. Thanks, however, to the determined efforts of groups of railway enthusiasts interested in preservation, among them the Main Line Steam Trust at Loughborough, and the Quainton Railway Society in Buckinghamshire, part at least of the GCR still lives on.

My own interest arose from the fact that its route had passed through my home village of Great Missenden. I began to read about its history and, over the years, walked along many miles of its sadly abandoned track bed to search out surviving features – viaducts, bridges, tunnels and stations – and soon acquired a nostalgia for this monument to an eminent Victorian, Sir Edward Watkin.

Previous accounts of the GCR have tended to concentrate on the construction of the line and the engineering feats which this involved, or have been based on reminiscences of its operation, or were fundamentally pictorial essays. Most illustrations have, in fact, come from the well-known S.W.A. Newton collection. In the present work, however, I have been able to include many new, unpublished photographs from other sources, some of which illustrate the line in its present day appearance. The text covers not only the development of the GCR but includes observations on social and demographic changes brought about by its construction and operation. One of the immediate consequences was a drift away from agriculture and the growth of railway towns such as Woodford Halse. Indeed, until the coming of the GCR, many villages and towns in central England had remained the same as in feudal times. As an avoiding line it played an important part in the two world wars providing for the movement of troops, munitions and raw materials.

LIST OF STATIONS

NAME	DATE OPENED	DATE CLOSED
Sheffield (Victoria)	15 Sept 1851	5 Jan 1970
Beighton	15 March 1899	1 Nov 1954
Staveley Central	15 March 1899	4 March 1963
Kirkby Bentinck	15 March 1899	4 March 1963
Hollin Well and Annesley	15 March 1899	4 March 1963
Hucknall Town	15 March 1899	4 March 1963
Bulwell Common	15 March 1899	4 March 1963
New Basford	15 March 1899	7 Sept 1964
Carrington	15 March 1899	24 Sept 1928
Nottingham Victoria	15 March 1899	5 Sept 1966
Arkwright	15 March 1899	21 July 1967
Ruddington	15 March 1899	4 March 1963
Rushcliffe Halt	15 March 1899	4 March 1963
East Leake	15 March 1899	3 May 1969
Loughborough Central	15 March 1899	RO Steam Railway
Quorn & Woodhouse	15 March 1899	RO Steam Railway
Rothley	15 March 1899	RO Steam Railway
Belgrave & Birstall	15 March 1899	RO in progress by GCRS 1976 Ltd
Leicester Central	15 March 1899	3 May 1969
Whetstone	15 March 1899	4 March 1963
Ashby Magna	15 March 1899	3 May 1969
Lutterworth	15 March 1899	3 May 1969
Rugby Central	15 March 1899	3 May 1969
Braunston & Willoughby	15 March 1899	1 April 1957
Charwelton	15 March 1899	4 March 1963
Woodford Halse	15 March 1899	5 Sept 1966
Culworth	15 March 1899	29 Sept 1958
Helmdon	15 March 1899	4 March 1963
Brackley Central	15 March 1899	5 Sept 1966
Finmere	15 March 1899	4 March 1963
Calvert	15 March 1899	4 March 1963
Quainton Road	15 March 1899	4 March 1963
Marylebone	15 March 1899	Planned 12 May 1986

Closure dates refer to when the station ceased to be in use for passengers.

OTHER LINES OWNED OR JOINTLY RUN BY THE GREAT CENTRAL

NAME	DATE OPENED	COMPANIES	DATE CLOSED
1 Woodford Halse Banbury stations			
Chacombe Road	17 April 1911	GW/GC	6 Feb 1956
Eydon Road	1 Oct 1913	GW/GC	2 April 1956
2 Grendon Underwood Northolt stations			
Akeman Street	2 April 1906	GW/GC	7 July 1930
Wotton	2 April 1906	GW/GC	7 Dec 1953
Haddenham	2 April 1906	GW/GC	?/?/1963
Ilmer	2 April 1906	GW/GC	?/?/1963

All stations to Northolt from High Wycombe were built new by the GW/GC while the layout and gauge of the line was changed on the Wycombe–Aylesbury section. New stations were as follows:

Beaconsfield	2 April 1906	GW/GC	–
Seer Green	2 April 1906	GW/GC	–
Gerrards Cross	2 April 1906	GW/GC	–
Denham Golf Club	2 April 1906	GW/GC	–
Denham	2 April 1906	GW/GC	–
West Ruislip	2 April 1906	GW/GC	–
South Ruislip	2 April 1906	GW/GC	–
Northolt Park	2 April 1906	GW/GC	–
Sudbury Hill	2 April 1906	GW/GC	–
Sudbury & Harrow Road	2 April 1906	GW/GC	–
Wembley Complex	2 April 1906	GW/GC	–
3 Aylesbury–Quainton Verney Junction	23 Sept 1868	Met/GC	6 July 1936
4 Quainton–Brill	1872	Met/GC	2 Dec 1935

Opposite
Marylebone's first passenger train arriving from Manchester London Road, on 7 November, 1898 before the line was officially opened. The train is headed by a Pollit Class 11A 4-4-0 268.

'Forward'

FORWARD

Chapter One

'FORWARD'

The railway network in Britain owed its birth to the Industrial Revolution. The need to convey an ever-increasing volume of coal and other raw materials for industry, the availability of cast iron for rails and locomotive production and the development of steam engines, at first stationary and then providing traction, are all factors which contributed to the rise of this new form of transport.

A further important stimulus which would, independently, have brought about such a development, arose from the poor state of communications throughout Britain which, until the eighteenth century, had remained a basically agricultural society with little change since the Middle Ages. One contemporary writer vividly described the roads as 'still what God had left after the Flood'. In Northamptonshire the situation was particularly bad and roads soon became morasses in wet weather. Even in relatively good conditions journey times were long: for example the stage-coach took four days from York to London. Alternative means of transportation were urgently needed and engineers of the calibre of Thomas Telford addressed themselves to the problem. At first rivers, supplemented by man-made canals, eased the problem. In the nineteenth century canals were, in their turn, superseded by railways.

Two essential prerequisites for the development of a railway network were the need for a permanent way and for steam engines which could provide their own motive power or traction. At Ironbridge there survive from the eighteenth century cast iron rails which had replaced the earlier wooden ones, along which wagons were drawn by horses. Wooden rails had in fact had a long history of use in mines from as early as the fifteenth century. Horsepower gave way to more efficient stationary engines which hauled trucks up and down inclined planes (Hay incline). Meanwhile Trevithick and the Stephensons built the prototypes of the modern steam locomotive.

The new era of railways had begun.

At first only freight was carried but a combined passenger and freight service was opened between Stockton and Darlington in 1825. This was followed by the Liverpool & Manchester Railway in 1830. The availability of money for investment (speculative finance) in the 1830s and 40s bore fruit in what is commonly referred to as 'railway mania'. The highwater mark was the year 1841 when no less than 270 Railway Bills received the Royal Assent.

Ten years later there were already 6,802 route miles in operation and, in the following fifty years this mileage was increased to 22,078. During this period the government reacted against the policy of *laissez-faire*, in other words, of continuing to allow private companies to develop independently of any State supervision. Its attitude had undoubtedly been coloured by its experience in dealing with the canal companies in previous years. However, far from promoting an integrated system, the government encouraged competition between rival groups because it feared the possible effects of a monopoly. Different ventures sprang up all over Britain wherever promoters thought they stood to make a worthwhile profit: the provision of the new form of transport as a 'public service' was a secondary consideration. One obvious repercussion of such uncoordinated development was that towns and villages often had more than one station even where there was only justification for one; for example, at Helmdon, Brackley and Wotton on the Great Central. Government participation in this essentially 'private industry' was limited except that, in 1844, the Board of Trade set up a committee under Lord Dalhousie to examine proposed railway schemes, the status of their promoters, possible national or local advantages of projected new lines, engineering problems involved in their construction and, finally, their cost and economic viability. It is, however, evident that such criteria were not always taken into account. It has been said, and rightly so: 'The interference of the State in a sphere where purely economic considerations alone were involved, was a landmark in the momentous conversion of the business community from the rigid doctrine of non-intervention.' The logical conclusion of that policy, many years later, led to the nationalisation of the railways. In 1888 Parliament passed the 'Railway and Canal Traffic Act'. At that time Edward, (later Sir Edward) Watkin, one of the greatest of the railway magnates of the late Victorian era, was already negotiating the development of a new line, the Great Central.

Edward Watkin, born in 1819, in Ravald St Salford, was one of three sons of Absalom Watkin, a wealthy Lancashire cotton merchant and respected citizen who had been connected with the Anti-Corn Law League. By a strange coincidence he was born in the same year as George Stephenson. His brothers John and Alfred became, respectively, vicar of Stoxwold and mayor of Manchester (1873–4). Edward entered his father's business and soon also became interested in public affairs.

He was at one time director of the Manchester Athenaeum and organised literary soirées. Watkin, in common with other prosperous Victorians, for example Thomas Holloway and Lord Shaftesbury, involved himself in philanthropic schemes, though on a modest scale. As Secretary of a fund-raising committee, he saw three public parks opened in 1845. Meanwhile his literary and business interest – he was by then a partner in his father's mill – led him to found the *Manchester Examiner*.

At the age of twenty-six Watkin had already begun his lifelong interest in railways, having become Secretary of the Trent Valley company. After a visit to the USA in 1851, an account of which be published on his return two years later, Watkin obtained his first major position as general manager of the Manchester, Sheffield & Lincolnshire Railway, under Huish. This was a turning point in his career and the Manchester, Sheffield & Lincolnshire became a keystone in his great railway empire. Watkin deserted his old

Sir Edwin Watkin, Chairman and founder of the London Extension of the MS&L, which became Great Central in 1897. He actually retired from the railway business in 1894 before the London Extension, his final dream could get under way and it was for this reason that the Great Central ended up building it in a different way to what he had really planned. Watkin was born in 1819 and died in 1901 in his eighty-second year.

Sir Douglas and Francis Fox, the engineers of the line who were noted for their viaducts at Brackley and tunnels at Catesby.

ally in favour of negotiating an arrangement with the Great Northern to give him running rights into London, and became Chairman of the South Eastern and the Metropolitan Railway (the earliest underground system). In addition, Watkin was also president of the Canadian Grand Trunk Railway. Unfortunately in spite of his negotiations, the Great Northern, North Western and Midland Railways all threatened disaster to his Great Central plan because he did not foresee the extent to which these rival companies would undermine the profitability of his own operations. In 1861, at the wish of the Duke of Newcastle, Watkin again travelled to North America, this time to Canada, on government business: he was sent to investigate means by which the then five British states could be combined to create a Dominion. He considered the first possibility of transferring the Hudson Bay company to government control, an expedient which was actually adopted in 1869. A further scheme was envisaged by Watkin by which Quebec would be connected with other Canadian ports on the Atlantic coast.

As Chairman of the Manchester Sheffield link, Watkin assumed full control on 27 January 1864 when he was forty-five. By then, because of his expertise and enterprise in matters relating to railways, Watkin was already considered as highly as George Hudson, the great railway king who, two decades earlier, had more than 1,000 miles of railway under his control and had been elected MP for Sunderland. The Manchester Sheffield line incorporated many smaller companies like the Cheshire; Midland; the Manchester South Junction and Atrincham; the Marple, New Mills and Hayfield Junction; and the Stockport and Woodley Junction.

In 1866 Watkin became a director of the Great Western and in the following year gained a position with the Great Eastern. He was also destined to control the South Eastern, Metropolitan and East London. Thus Watkin, by strategically acquiring various companies, began to lay the foundations for the fulfilment of his dream – the construction of a railway from Liverpool to Paris through London and a Channel tunnel link.

In 1877 Watkin built the Manchester & Liverpool Railway and, in 1892, thought about extending the Metropolitan northwards out of Buckinghamshire into Northamptonshire to Moreton Pinkney. Also, as part of his growing empire, a line was built between north and south Wales, including the Mersey tunnel which allowed a rail connection with Lancashire to be established.

Watkin's schemes, however, were not restricted to this country and one of his most interesting involvements was with the electrified railway from Athens to the Piraeus.

In 1845 Watkin married Mary Briggs (d. 1887) and of this marriage there was a son, Alfred Mellor Watkin, who became MP for Grimsby and director of the Manchester, Sheffield & Lincolnshire Railway from 1875–7 and 1899 onwards; and a daughter, Harriette, who married Worsley Taylor of Moreton Hall, Whaley. His second wife, Anne Little, died in 1896, three years after they were married. Watkin himself died in 1901 and his ultimate ambition – the construction of a Channel tunnel – was never fulfilled.

Watkin's predecessor, John Chapman, whose protégé he had once been, was markedly different in character but was a supporter of his. Chapman was a patient negotiator and basically of easygoing temperament, whereas Watkin was a commanding ambitious entrepreneur. In politics they belonged to different parties. Chapman was Conservative MP for Grimsby from 1862–5 and 1874 until his death in 1870. Watkin, by contrast, was a staunch Liberal, MP for Gt Yarmouth 1857–8; Stockport 1864–8; and Hythe 1874–95; after which he became an independent Liberal Unionist. Both men shared a common interest in the literary and public world, and were leading lights in the campaign for Saturday half-holidays. They became magistrates and ultimately Deputy Lieutenant and

The poster says it all about the railway's purpose and intentions, giving an insight into where one could go.

High Sheriff-Chapman in 1855 and Watkin some years later. However, in spite of their wealth, position and influence, they were unable to achieve for their shareholders in the MS&L more than a 3.1/2% dividend on ordinary shares. This poor return led detractors to nickname the line 'Money Sunk and Lost', while some travellers referred to it as 'Muck, Sludge and Lightning' because of the area through which it went.

Watkin's dream had involved two major projects, a Channel tunnel and a line from the North of England into London. Since the

negotiations with the directors of the Great Northern were unsuccessful, although they had formerly been his allies, Sir Edward resolved to follow the practice of the Midland which made use of 'rented lines'. He failed, however, to take into consideration the changed financial situation: when indeed the Midland had made their decision, the railways were in an era of prosperity and expansion. At the time of the MS&L, the boom period for the birth of new lines was already over and this particular line was far from a prosperous concern like the rival Great North-

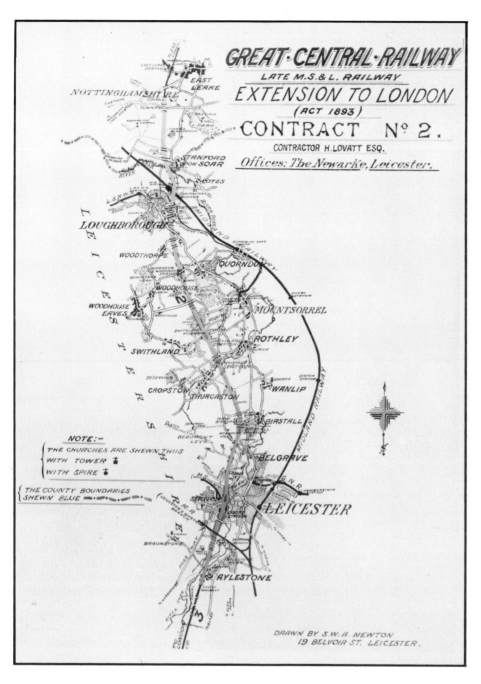

Diagram showing the extent of Contract No. 2.

believed that it would be better to start afresh rather than attempt to patch up existing systems which were unable to cope. Sir Edward, however, failed to take into consideration the invention of the 'horseless carriage' and its likely effect on the long-term development of the railways even though the full impact was not felt until the construction of motorways after the Second World War. Watkin also claimed that the Great Central would be a positive benefit to London since it would transport more important supplies like milk, coal, timber and food generally from the counties through which it passed. Three coalfields also lay unworked, he argued, because of the lack of a rail network to serve them. Baron Ferdinand de Rothschild, then MP for mid-Bucks, who lived at Waddesdon Manor (also the name of one of the stations) came forward to support Sir Edward, suggesting that the proposed line would bring about a considerable improvement in local communications which had previously been very poor. At Braunston, Colonel Henry Lowndes thought that a direct line to Leicester would be a booster for the local shoe industry and would lead to an increase in the manufacture of other commodities. Nevertheless, the population statistics of the preceding census had shown a drop of 100 in the number of villagers in Braunston. Many cynics observed that the fox cover was the most profitable venture in the village at that time.

Public opinion has always been a crucial factor in the choice of routes for railways but in Buckinghamshire, the local landlords and prominent figures in society seem to have been carried away by the idea that the Great Central was intended purely for their use. The traders welcomed it as a new facility. Two further factors determined the nature and, ultimately, the economic viability of the Great Central. The main occupations of the heart of England were dependent on agriculture, and labourers had no reason to travel beyond their village, and even if they had had the inclination, the fares would have been prohibitive.

ern and Midland. The latter two companies believed, quite rightly, that a third route would be completely superfluous and therefore uneconomic, since the major towns were already served by the existing network of railways. Thus the route for the MS&L virtually predetermined and lay through the heart of England which, at that time, was mainly agricultural and consisted of a number of small villages. Watkin's logical argument for the construction of the new line was that there would be sufficient growth in traffic to justify such a route as the Great Central. He further asserted that the other companies would need to expand and improve their lines. He further

Because of the major engineering works and disruption involved there was active opposition to the new line, mainly from artists living in the St John's Wood colony, and the Marylebone Cricket Club since Lords itself was threatened. A petition was organised at the London end, the protest being directed against the proposed goods depot which would swallow up 35 acres of land: the depot was to handle coal, fish, manure and other commodities considered undesirable for such an area. Opposition from the cricketers, however, posed the more serious threat and W. G. Grace led the protest in person. Sir Edward reacted without delay because it appeared that his Railway Bill was in grave danger of being rejected by Parliament. He agreed quickly to a compromise: his new line would be hidden by a tunnel and, when the construction work was completed, the pitch at Lords would be restored to its former condition. This was acceptable. At St John's Wood, however, opposition continued and the case for the MS&L was undertaken by Ralph Littler CB, QC. The hearing opened on 17 April 1891 and lasted fifteen days. Parliament failed to come to any decision. Watkin, undaunted by this, pushed to get the bill read a second time. By the end of March in the following year the MS&L was revived

and the only objections left were against the siting of the terminus (Marylebone) and a railway hotel in Boscabel Gardens. Properties were bought and demolished: the way was now clear.

On 12 April, after a further fortnight's sitting, the Committee approved most of the plan for the construction of the Great Central and, after six more days, agreed to the other outstanding points. The proposals of the MS&L were accepted by the House of Lords. A further hitch occurred when Lord Salisbury dissolved Parliament and it was not until July, when Gladstone took office, that the final consent was given. Royal permission for the Bill was received on 28 March 1893. Meanwhile the Metropolitan had extended its line as far as Aylesbury (1 September 1892): there it connected with the Aylesbury & Buckingham Railway which ended at Verney Junction, the station built for the local landowner and Deputy Chairman of the Aylesbury & Buckingham Railway, Sir Harry Verney.

The Metropolitan intended to extend its line from Quainton to Moreton Pinkney, 24½ miles distant, in order to help the MS&L create a junction with the East and West Junction Railway near the site of the future Woodford Halse station. The MS&L resolved to build the line the whole way from Beighton in Sheffield, to

Signboard near Western Road, Leicester, heralding the opening of the new line. Boards like this were erected at various intervals along the route. This particular board was at the rear of the royal Show Ground and was photographed in June 1896, a year before the title Great Central was adopted for Sir Edward Watkin's large railway network. Although building of the line commenced in 1894, the title Great Central was not adopted until the London Extension was well under way.

Quainton Road in Buckinghamshire, where it would meet the Metropolitan at a junction near Upper South Farm, thus abandoning the idea of extending the Metropolitan. Many factors were eventually to frustrate the fulfilment of Sir Edward Watkin's dream of a railway from Manchester to Paris, but for the moment the way was at last clear for Sir Edward to forge ahead with the construction of the London Extension which was an essential part of his grand design.

Like any large-scale civil engineering project, however, the construction of the Great Central Railway involved a number of serious problems. The proposed route, about which there was little or no room for manoeuvre, was bound to cause disruption in the already built-up towns and cities and dispossession of some workers from their homes. Moreover, it would drive a 'swathe' through the farmlands of Nottinghamshire, Leicestershire, Northamptonshire and Buckinghamshire. Physical problems arising from the nature of the terrain compounded manmade difficulties: in their turn, canals, rivers, roads and other main lines provided obstacles which had to be crossed or circumvented. Where the route lay through the densely populated cities of Nottingham, Leicester and Rugby, major engineering works in the form of bridges, viaducts and tunnels were necessary to carry the track. But, not the least of the many difficulties facing Watkin was the raising of the finance necessary for this ambitious project. The economic situation was, indeed, very different from that of the earlier years of railway development.

Although British railway companies existed and operated under normal business rules of cost effectiveness and profit, the Great Central company was, from the outset, granted two unusual public privileges, namely corporate status and the power to acquire property by compulsory purchase. In spite of this, however, work on the line was delayed by a number of com-

One of the contractors' depots along the line. Note the grand design of the shed and the artistic lettering on the barge boards. The rails in the foreground are part of the contractor's railway which was used to transport the heavy machinery and materials needed for the construction of the railway.

plicated battles over land purchase. Some of the land in question had a high amenity value, as, for example, Lords cricket ground. When estates were involved elsewhere, as at Woodford and Catesby, there was a conflict of interests, as it was felt that the route was likely to disturb the environment and cause annoyance to land-owners: protracted negotiations ensued and some diversions from the route, or other expedients, were necessary.

Eventually, by September 1894, all seven contracts had been agreed for a total of £3,132,155, together with a provision of £250,000 for the Channel tunnel project. Kellett analyses the motives behind railway investment as follows: 'In general the choice of routes, sites and parti-cular operational policies was made privately and according to the ordi-nary calculations of profitability and investment which prevailed in a *laissez-faire* economy. The rail-way companies were business enter-prises floated with private capital: in the long run their success and survival depended upon the return they were able to give their share-holders. The paramount consider-ation, therefore, in the minds of projectors and managers of Britain's nineteenth-century railway system when making decisions was a rela-tively simple one: what balance could be expected between the direct private costs and benefits of the investment. The Victorian entrepreneur was guided by experi-ence and common sense raised to a very high order, not by systems anaylsis.'

Judged by such criteria, Watkin's shareholders in the Great Central were involved in a very poor invest-ment which paid only 3% on ordinary shares compared, for example, with the high dividend of 60% paid by the Midland Rail-way company.

Watkin's budget, however, extended in fact to four times his original estimate – a phenomenon of costing far from unknown in modern times – and reached a total of £11,500,000.

In order to bring the MS&L to London, authorisation was given for eleven sections of line. The first four covered the route between

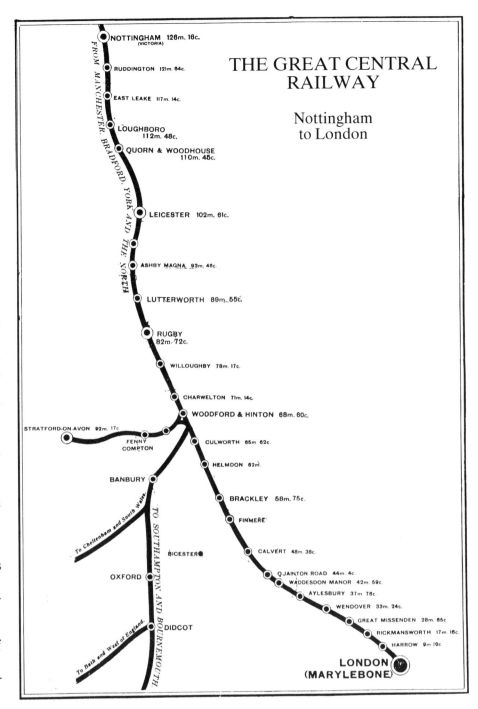

THE GREAT CENTRAL RAILWAY

Nottingham to London

Annesley and Quainton Road. The fifth was a link line with the London North Western Railway in the parish of Clifton-upon-Dunsmore. The sixth and seventh contracts were two junctions with the East and West Junction Railway at a site south of Woodford. The eighth was for a junction with the Metro-politan at Canfield Place to Marylebone (2 miles 20 chains). The ninth referred to a section where the line was widened be-tween Willesden and Hampstead (1 mile 69 chains). The eleventh and twelfth were for the provision of a coal-yard branch (35½ chains in length), and a connection to the Inner Circle line west of Baker

Street driving under the plot for the Great Central hotel (37 chains). Strangely there is no mention of a tenth section. It is possible that this was the line through the Channel tunnel, or indeed a line across London to join with a route to the south coast: the latter seems more likely.

The total cost of the contracts was £3,132,155 divided up as fol-lows among seven contractors:

Contract	Mileage	Contractor	Cost (£)
(1) Annesley–East Leake	19m 44ch	Logan & Hemmingway, Market Harborough.	668,451
(2) East-Leake–Aylestone	16m 36ch	H. Lovatt, Northampton	548,835
(3) Aylestone–Rugby	15m 69ch	Topham, Jones, Railton, Westminster.	281,589
(4) Rugby–Charwelton	15m 77ch	Toliver & Son, Horsham, Sussex.	513,308
(5) Charwelton–Brackley	12m 32ch	Walter Scott, Newcastle-on-Tyne.	
(6) Brackley–Quainton Road	12m 61ch	Walter Scott, Newcastle-on-Tyne.	420,000
(7) London–Marylebone (Canfield Place)	1m 71ch	J. T. Firbank, London Bridge.	699,972
	94m 70ch		£3,132,155

Navvy Missionary and Mission room at Loughborough. Note the simple interior with its wooden benches, altar, and posters depiciting scenes from the Bible. The organist is seen practising in readiness for a service.

A group of navvies with their wives and children dressed in their Sunday best, with a large banner proclaiming Calvert Navvy Mission Sunday School. Note the band at the tail-end of the procession with the tubas and the large drum.

Taken on a sunny afternoon, the typical dwelling of a navvy: a wooden hut with a couple of rooms containing bedroom and living area. The cast iron 'John Bull' stove provided heating, cooking facilities and a drying area. The furniture is basic with very little luxury, apart from the carpet, gas light and pictures on the wall.

The actual construction work began with tremendous enthusiasm and high expectations: Lord Wharncliffe cut the first turf at Alpha Road, near Lords cricket ground, on 13 November 1894. Since the early days of the railways many innovations have been made in the field of civil engineering. A major advance was the introduction of new earth-shifting equipment – steam-driven mechanical excavators. In spite of this, however, many tasks still relied on the tireless efforts of the navvy and his muscle power, and to maintain his strength would eat as much as two pounds of meat and drink a gallon of ale at a single meal!

The navvy and his kind, although widely believed to be uncouth and irreligious, were often responsible and God-fearing men, as was demonstrated by the arrival of new religious sects, among them Moravians and Methodists. A Navvy Mission Society was created and huts were set up with the aim of encouraging the navvies to go there and pray. Inside were hard seats, a stove, harmonium, and texts nailed to the walls. If the navvies could not attend, the Mission would go to the site where they were working. Under such influences the navvy gradually became more civilised and no longer terrorised the countryside. However, there were exceptions, since ungodliness dies hard, and these tended to confirm the view of

Victorian moralists who still believed that the navvy was unregenerate.

As the railway became established the Moravians settled themselves in Woodford where they built their own church and a graveyard in the 'rural area'. They also built a church at Eydon which was later to be an outpost of the GC. The Moravians themselves were a Christian community founded in Eastern Bohemia. They laid great store by purity of morals and, being convinced that the Church was corrupted, set up societies in Moravia and Bohemia. Followers were known as brethren of Chelic and wore distinctive dress. They accepted the Bible as their only standard of faith and their doctrine was generally broad and radical. They taught the Apostles' Creed, rejected purgatory, the worship of Saints and the authority of the Catholic Church. The Moravians had begun their work in England after the Methodist John Wesley and his brother were converted to the Religion. Each railway settlement had its own church and clergyman, as, for example, at Neasden, Sheffield and Annesley.

Annesley, the commencement of the line, contained a large marshalling yard, a six-road engine shed capable of accommodating thirty locomotives, repair shops and an electricity supply. There the line joined with the Great Northern to Sheffield. The first

Carrington Station site looking north into Sherwood Rise tunnel which is newly completed judging by the date on the key stone: 1896. The lines in place are contractors lines and work is already beginning on cutting away the sandstone to build the platforms and retaining walls. On the far left is one of the works trains containing a covered wagon which was used for tool storage. The spire on top of the tunnel is that of Sherwood Rise church.

The south end of Mansfield Road tunnel burrowed under Woodborough Road after leaving the station at Nottingham Victoria which lay in a deep pit carved out of the rock. Here the formers are still in place just inside the tunnel while the running lines are ready for trains. The site on the left in this 1897 picture is being prepared for the turntable which, like its counterpart at the south end, was barely long enough to take large express engines when the line opened.

large-scale work involved driving a cutting through the limestone and magnesium rock at Hucknall. No less than 27,000 cubic yards of spoil were excavated by mechanical shovels and with the aid of explosives. Some 2½ miles to the south, at Bulwell, a viaduct was constructed to pass over the Mansfield line which belonged to the Midland. This consisted of twenty-six arches, some skew, and was 420 yards in length. To the north of Bulwell, junctions were formed again with the Great Northern, Leen Valley and Derby lines. At Basford station a carriage lighting works was built similar to those at Leicester and Marylebone, supplying gas for 500 coaches. At Nottingham the MS&L encountered its first major problems since large-scale tunnelling was necessary at Sherwood Rise (665 yards), Mansfield Road, (1,189 yards), Victoria Street (398 yards) and Thurland Street. Between Sherwood and Mansfield tunnels, Carrington station was built with the intention of attracting commuters from the surrounding area. Between Mansfield and Victoria Street, the new joint Victoria station was constructed.

Victoria Street tunnel posed an extremely difficult set of problems because the roof was likely to undermine several house foundations and to break into cellars and vaults. Many buildings had to be shored up while excavations were in progress. When the old Guildhall was demolished, the navvies found bodies of executed criminals who were then reburied in another piece of unhallowed ground. In Victoria Street the tunnel hit the vault of the local bank and the MS&L had to replace the building and safe. There was a lighter side, however, when the thirsty navvies accidentally broke into the cellars of the 'Dog and Partridge' and the old 'Cross Keys', and consumed part of the stocks. At the southern end of the tunnel was Weekday Cross Junction whence the Great Northern ran into Midland Road. At the end of the junction was a 52-arched viaduct and 12 steel bridges which ran for ⅝ mile, passing over the Midland and its sidings. The next construction was a station which had access to Arkwright Street, from which

it derived its name. From that point forward, the line quadrupled and there was a large locomotive shed with a capacity of 16 engines, coal depot, goods warehouse and freight yard complete with travelling crane. The river Trent, south of Nottingham, provided the next obstacle and this was crossed by a girder span of 66 feet, three brick arches and three lattice girders of 112 feet each, followed by seven further arches. At East Leake the line reverted to two tracks running through the countryside – with a station at Ruddington, a small village south of Nottingham. Near Ruddington a branch left the London extension to Gotham. A cutting involved the removal of 320,000 cubic yards of soil at East Leake. This completed the first contract in the northern division carried out by Logan & Hemmingway.

Contract (2) began with a tunnel (99 yards) and a cutting through shale which necessitated the removal of 300,000 cubic yards of spoil. Before the station at Loughborough there was an

Weekday Cross from the south end of Thurland Street tunnel, the 'up' running line is in position for London while work is in hand on installing the connection to the Grantham line which was worked by Great Northern line trains. The signal cabin is also nearing completion and one signal has been installed. Under the signal are the rooftops of Drury Hill, and above on the left is Garners Hill. At this stage the line was three years away from completion.

21

Drury Hill, Nottingham, during the upheaval of the railway construction where several properties have already been demolished to allow the line to be carried through the city on a series of viaducts. Up above, in the shadow, is Garners Hill and Weekday Cross where the railway branched off to the Grantham line. The imposing church and surrounding buildings have altered little, although the cobbled street and its buildings have now disappeared. Drury Hill is now Middle Hill, while the Broad Marsh which went off to the left of the picture is now part of a huge shopping centre.

Part of the viaduct over Swithland reservoir as seen from Brazil Island which lay in the middle of the vast expanse of water. When the two viaducts were being built the whole reservoir was drained and then refilled. Swithland supplied water for the city of Leicester and was one of the most beautiful spots on the line.

embankment built up to 40–50 feet and two viaducts were needed, the first 160 yards in length with 11 arches; the second, a skew girder bridge crossing a canal and the railway between Leicester and Loughborough. The platform at Loughborough Central is of interest; like many others on the Great Central, it was based on the island principle and access to it was provided by a stairway from the road. Near the station a goods depot was built.

After Loughborough the line entered different terrain, hilly, heavily wooded, and with reservoirs. The line passed through Quorn, Woodhouse and Charnwood forest. At Swithland there were sidings but the projected station never materialised. The reservoir was crossed by two viaducts of five and ten arches respectively (each of 30 feet span) and a plate girder bridge (40 feet span). Nearby, a private branch line served the granite quarries at Montsorrel. Island-platform stations were constructed at Rothley, Belgrave and Birstall.

Leicester provides an interesting example of a further way in which the line negotiated a heavily built-up area. Whereas in Nottingham a series of tunnels had been driven, here the line relied on a viaduct, basically of brick arches together with fine examples of girder bridges. At least 300 houses had to be demolished to make way for the Great Central. In addition, even the goods yards, and station were sited above ground-level. The station, again built on the island principle had two bays at either end; nearby, a parcels depot and 'stabling point' for locomotives. Leicester engine shed situated half a mile south of the station could accommodate 30 engines with appropriate maintenance facilities. Further sidings for sorting coal wagons were sited at Abbey Lane. The Leicester corporation improved access to the station by a 200,000 road-widening scheme. Aylestone with its viaduct over the Leicester canal, marked the end of the second contract. The Great Central actually crossed the canal, or river Soar, six times on its route through Leicester. During the construction of the station and associated work,

Apart from the massive crossing which had to be made over the Midland station at Nottingham, the river Trent also had to be crossed at Wilford Road by this multiple variation of structures. The contractors line on the right crossed by a temporary wooden structure to bring materials to help build the goods station, sited on the spot in the foreground. When this picture was taken the embankment was being formed by earth dumped from tipplers. Further along the viaduct on the lattice girder stretch a steam locomotive simmers gently.

Belgrave and Birstall in the final stages of completion. The running lines are in and buildings are ready. All that remains to be done is the surfacing of the platform and painting of the wooden station name. Belgrave was one of those island platforms whose access was made via a staircase from the road above. Worthy of note is the extra building third along from the road bridge.

Leicester Central, like nearly all the other stations along the line, was built on an island between 'up' and 'down' tracks with bays at either end to accommodate local workings to Nottingham and Rugby. This picture shows the partially completed awning over the main platforms and the north end bays. Under the main part of the platform, part of a Roman pavement was covered up and preserved and this was accessible from Blackfriars Street, which lay below the 'down' main line.

Leicester Central engine shed under construction. In this plate the doors are being assembled with the aid of a primitive rail crane and scaffolding. Behind the hut and the truck in the foreground is the site of the offices for the shedmaster.

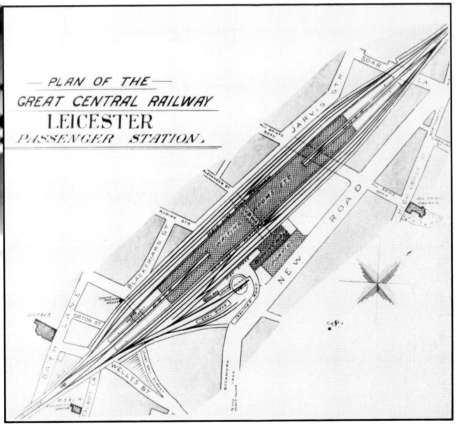

PLAN OF THE
GREAT CENTRAL RAILWAY
LEICESTER
PASSENGER STATION.

Diagram of Leicester Central and its environs.

Left
A rather happy bunch of station staff pose for a picture in the booking hall of Leicester Central station shortly after the line opened. The man with the poster is sitting on top of a platform trolley loaded with parcels, while the man to the right in the bowler hat is probably the stationmaster.

Opposite top
The bridge over Western Boulevard near Braunston Gate which was built on a skew formation. The picture shows clearly the cross girders which bore the trackbed. Note the steam crane and the gantry, also the deep bed in the foreground for the ballast and gravel levels.

Opposite bottom
Lutterworth station, as seen from the 'down' side of the platform. The glass shelter nearest the photographer covered the stairway from the road below. The space under the name Lutterworth was used for poster display. The little window under the clock in the first building is the ticket office.

Below
The Rugby 'Birdcage' bridge, (so named because of its construction) seen here from the Hillmorton side, crossed the fourteen tracks of the London North Western Railway and the Avon canal. Note the little group of spectators leaning up against the fence, giving them a bird's eye view of both lines.

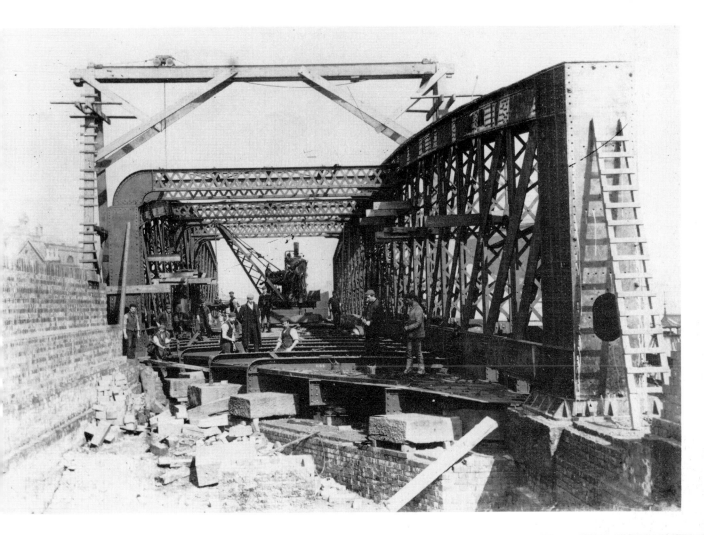

many Roman finds were made including a pavement, which was subsequently specially preserved and encased for public viewing.

The last contract in the northern division extended to Rugby Central. In this section were three stations, Whetstone, Ashby Magna and Lutterworth. Among major works needed were the bank at Whetstone which took eighteen months to complete, and a thirteen-arched viaduct over the river Fence. The Leicester to Nuneaton line was crossed just south of the viaduct by a skew plate girder bridge: a link was made at this point with the Midland Railway for the transportation of stone from the local quarries.

South of Ashby Magna the line plunged into a cutting leading to the tunnel at Dunton Bassett (92 yards long). The final project was the construction of a five-arched skew viaduct to carry the road across the railway at Rugby.

The southern section began with a four-span viaduct across the Oxford canal which led to an embankment built up with

LUTTERWORTH STATION

3,000,000 cubic yards of earth and gravel. To cross the Midland main lines and sidings, fourteen arches, a steel bridge comprising two plates (58 and 75 feet long respectively) three lattice girder bridges (105, 165 and 105 feet long) and a plate girder bridge (40 feet) were needed: the girder construction was nicknamed the 'birdcage' because of its shape and appearance. The crossing, however, blocked the view of the London North Western Railway's signal box, so a new signal gantry had to be provided by the Great Central. South of this complex, after a cutting of 1¾ miles, was Rugby Central. The proximity of the canal and the line for a distance of 2¾ miles, greatly facilitated the transport of building materials, just as did the connection with the Daventry-Leamington link. The latter was crossed south of Willoughby by a viaduct of thirteen arches.

The major difficulties south of Willoughby were caused by the Northamptonshire uplands and rivers. The Leam, the first river, was crossed at Staverton by a nine-arched viaduct and again at Catesby by a twelve-arched viaduct constructed from local Northamptonshire stone. At Catesby the most noticeable feature was the tunnel which was built solely to obscure the view of steam trains at the insistence of the owners of Catesby House, which had originally

Top
The northern portal of Catesby tunnel in the early stages of construction by Thomas Oliver & Son, the contractors. The rough and ready rails laid into the tunnel were used to extract the vast quantities of soil from the tunnel, while on the left lie the massive heaps of engineer's blue bricks used to face the tunnel. Behind the line of trees lay the home of Robert Catesby, the gunpowder plotter.

Centre
Ready for the first trains, an immaculate Rugby Central stands deserted. In design Rugby was akin to the island-platform layout at Loughborough, which also had a large booking office at street level. The picture is looking north to the LNWR station from the 'up' side of the platform.

Bottom
The luxury end of accommodation Great Central style! Here Braunston and Willoughby's stationmaster poses in front of his house one fine summer day. Like the garden, the house was fairly spacious.

belonged to one of the participants in the Gunpowder Plot. The tunnel in fact replaced what was to have been a 3,000-yard-long cutting. Restrictions were placed on the positioning of the ventilation shafts and the four breathers were cleverly disguised, being built of blue bricks faced with mortar and cement where water was likely to seep. At the southern end of the tunnel a cutting was excavated and involved the removal of 410,000 cubic yards of earth.

At Charwelton a small station was built and a marshalling yard. This latter feature, usually only found at larger stations, was necessary because the line met a tramway to a nearby quarry. South of Charwelton the track carried water-troughs were supplied from a large water tower.

The final major work included in contract (4) was the provision of a new station and houses at Woodford Halse soon to accommodate a whole railway community. South of the station was the junction with the East & West Junction Railway which consisted of two curves north and south, the former for a link with Woodford, the latter to provide

trains from Marylebone with a through connection to Stratford-upon-Avon. At this point the last two contracts began, both carried out by Walter Scott & Company, for the section of the Great Central as far as Quainton Road.

The first station was Culworth which served the small village: to the south at Sulgrave an embankment was built containing 486,000 cubic yards of spoil. The bank was 48 feet high with slopes of 1/8, 340 feet wide at its base, and covered an area of approximately 17 acres of what had formerly been good agricultural land. A temporary brickworks was set up to supply bricks for stations, viaducts and bridges: in all some 12 million bricks were produced at this yard. The Helmdon valley was crossed by a nine-arched viaduct under which went the Northampton & Banbury Junction Railway. Helmdon station had a simple island platform since Watkin thought that this would allow more space for quadrupling the tracks when the Channel tunnel had been completed.

Brackley was the next major centre served by the new line and the digging-out of the approach

A typical country scene of the summer: a motley collection of farm workers involved in threshing take a well-earned break to pose for Sidney Newton and his camera near Charwelton. Note the boy with the yoke on his back, next to the dog. The threshing engine was steam-powered and probably maintained by the man in the dark overalls by the steam gauge.

29

Woodford Halse Junction. The curve off
to the left came in from Byfield and
Stratford-on-Avon and ran in to a wooden
platform in the main station complex which
was used by these local trains, and later by
the trains to Banbury which used the
Culworth route. The extent of the
trackwork was phenomenal and the
marshalling yards were known as 'The
Pride of Europe'.

Another view of Woodford, this time a
family shot with the stationmaster, adorned
in his uniform, and his wife and children,
who appear dressed up specially for the
occasion. Note the clothing and short hair
styles, so commonplace in Victorian times.

Walter Scott & Co's contractors' depot and camp. The huts in the background are the navvies quarters, while in the foreground are the sidings and raw materials to build the line. The line through the centre is that of the Northampton and Banbury Junction Railway. The stack of bricks were for the viaduct at Helmdon, the piers of which can be seen in the lefthand corner of the picture.

Woodford Halse station, with the smart stationmaster almost standing to attention with a message paper in his hand. Similar uniforms can be seen today on the preserved section of the Great Central at Loughborough Central, Quorn or Rothley. Behind the stationmaster is the footbridge over to platform 3 used for local trains. The platform in the picture is the 'down' main while the signal cabin in the background controlled the junction and the entrance to the goods yard.

Above
Dinner break at Brackley viaduct.

Opposite top
Calvert station under the second stage of construction. The roadbridge is complete and the hole for the staircase is ready. The platform is being levelled off for facing and surfacing and the foundations of the buildings are being laid.

Opposite bottom
Quainton Road Junction for the Metropolitan Railway which branched off to the right to Verney Junction and the Wotton Tramway which left from platform 3 of the station. The box on the left was provided by the Metropolitan for the junction with the London Extension which came in under the left of the two bridges. The picture here shows the junction in June 1897, two years before the line opened.

cuttings was a considerable undertaking (800,000 cubic yards). South of the station was the river Ouse bridged by a 23-arched viaduct. The last two arches were reinforced plate girders to prevent subsidence as the subsoil beneath the line was liable to move under the weight of the viaduct. At Finmere a wooden bridge was built for use by the hunt and the station was intended to serve Buckingham as well, but this was an unnecessary duplication since the LNWR already had a suitable site in the town itself. Likewise there was little point in the station at Calvert in view of the fact that there was no village nearby. The name of the station derived from the local landowner Sir Harry Verney who had been born a Calvert: the family estate was at Claydon. He dedi-

cated the station to the memory of his mother. Here also Itters & Company set private sidings for their brickworks.

At Upper South Farm, near Quainton, the line reached the Metropolitan which diverged to Verney junction at this point. The line crossed the tortuous route of the Metropolitan, continuing through Aylesbury, Great Missenden, Amersham and Rickmansworth to Canfield Place (Marylebone). An expansive complex was built at Neasden, a large site, which included a shed for 30 engines, a carriage and wagon shop, electric plant, tank house and offices. To accommodate railway employees 150 houses were built in the surrounding area. The last section of the Great Central began at Hampstead with tunnel-

Above the west coast main line at Loudon Road, near St John's Wood, between Lords tunnel and West Hampstead tunnel, there was a short gap provided for ventilation purposes. Both tunnels were built by the cut-and-cover method.

Taken from the girder bridge over the London North Western Railway, the buildings either side of the tunnel had been shored up to carry out work. To underpin these buildings a team of miners had to be brought in to work on what was probably the most exciting contract in the construction. The southern end of the tunnel was not without its problems, as it burrowed under Lords Cricket Ground, and because of the need to build by cut-and cover the pitch was removed and relaid when the work was complete, at the expense of the railway. In this picture the formers are still in position to hold up the north end of the tunnel.

ling: when the line came into the open it crossed the North Western at London Road by a girder bridge. A second tunnel was driven under St John's Wood and Lords cricket ground. The line passed under Rossmore Road and, before the terminus, branched off to a goods and coal depot and to a warehouse with the latest machinery. The most interesting piece of equipment was the 25-ton travelling crane.

Marylebone itself was built with four platforms serving five lines. Although the smallest of the London termini, it was noteworthy from an architectural point of view. The canopies covering the platforms were supported by an intricate system of columns and girders, except for Platform 4 which had a cantilever roof. The station was light and airy with an imposing façade and booking hall. There was a direct connection with the Underground from the concourse. Offices and Directors' board rooms completed the complex. Outside the station, a small locomotive

shed, carriage building, and lighting department to supply oil lamps for passenger trains were built.

Such were some of the main, distinctive features of the route, the problems which it faced and the engineering projects which successfully overcame them. It remains briefly to consider the actual trackwork.

The permanent way, of standard gauge track, was laid on a ballasted foundation of large rough stones mainly obtained from local quarries, with coarse gravel-graded two inch rings on top. It is estimated that about 750,000 cubic yards of stone were needed to ballast each mile of double track. The subsoil varied from area to area: the engineers made skilful use of burnt clay layers. In Northamptonshire ironstone slag from the ironworks was a readily available source of ballast.

In the trackwork, however, there was a strange anomaly in that, whereas other companies had used 60- and 45-feet lengths, the Great

Marylebone Station site after the area had been cleared and the retaining walls erected in readiness for the construction of the four-platformed terminus, note the contractors' wagons on the newly-laid running lines, inscribed with the name Joseph T. Firbank, who was the contractor for the line from Canfield Place to Marylebone.

The station frontage of Marylebone station in London North Eastern Railway days. Note the simple design of the facade and the rather grand gateway into the actual station complex. Note also the black London cab to the left of the picture under the canopy.

Central used 30-foot sections, thus changing the tradition of the MS&L.

A further interesting feature of the Great Central route was the complete absence of level crossings. This not only reduced hazards but allowed continuous operation.

Although the engineers had to drive their line 'across the grain of England and along the spine of the watershed', there is no gradient steeper than 1 in 176, no curve less than one mile in radius. Maintaining these exacting standards involved extensinve engineering works, as has been shown. The achievements of the Great Central engineers stands as a tribute to Victorian skill, independently of any consideration of the viability of the route as a commercial undertaking, or indeed of the need for its existence.

Opposite
Opening ceremony and departure of the first train to Manchester from Marylebone station on 9 March, 1899.

Openings and Alliances

FORWARD

Marylebone
Of all the termini, Marylebone was always best known for its light airy gentlemen's club-like atmosphere and it has changed little since its early days.

Chapter Two

THE 'OPENING OF THE LINE' AND THE 'ALLIANCE'

By 1897 work on the line was almost complete, except for the station at Nottingham (Victoria) and the Great Central Hotel, at Marylebone. Although the MS&L became incorporated in the new title Great Central, this name was not officially applied to the line until 9 March 1899. By the end of 1898 coal trains had already started running to 'wear in the track' and the terminus at Marylebone was nearing completion. The hotel, leased to Frederick Hotels, was built by Maple & Co and provided facilities for what was at that time a rather prosperous, high-class red-light quarter of London. After a chequered existence, requisitioned in both world wars by the government and War Department, in 1947, after the nationalisation of the railways, it became the head-quarters of the British Railways Board, 222 Marylebone Road. The MS&L had never actually owned the hotel but in the leasing agreement there was included a possible option to allow purchase by the Company should funds become available for this at a later date. The Company, however, had barely enough capital to complete Marylebone station itself and so the plans with regard to the hotel never came to fruition. The hotel, like the station, provided a striking 'monumentum' to a past age, a pleasant contrast to nearby high-rise buildings of glass and concrete of modern times!

The first passenger service, for Directors only, ran on 9 March, an occasion celebrated by a lavish dinner party, following in the tradition of Brunel and other noteworthy railway engineers of the Victorian era. The whole concourse together with the platform area provided the 'dining-room' which was elaborately decorated with flags.

Under the canopy
The opening of the line warranted a major celebration and the concourse was laid out for a big banquet for all the dignitaries connected with the inauguration of the Great Central. With all the bunting and decorations, it is hard to imagine that this is Marylebone Station.

Great Central Street
Nearing completion is the Hotel Grand Central which was commissioned for service on 1 July 1899, a few months after the opening of the station. One of its features was a cycle track on the roof which was useful for businessmen of the day to help them recover from high living. The area in which the hotel was situated was, at that time, the red-light quarter of London and many of the negotiators for the building of the line were known to have taken advantage of the ladies!

Marylebone
Another view of the inside of the main concourse showing old-fashioned advertisements for various wares and tobaccos. In the foreground is an artificial garden. A feature of the Great Central was the arrangement of ornamental gardens and the odd palm tree, used to brighten up the atmosphere.

Marylebone *Opposite*
A general view of the concourse in the early years. Note the typical Victorian dress as shown on the formidable lady in the front of the picture. The garden has gone but the newspaper stall and platform layout remains the same.

Ready for the off *Opposite bottom*
No. 861 stands with the first train whilst a crowd of impatient dignitaries wait for the magic moment. The special silver lever in the middle was pulled by Colonel Ritchie: this released the controls on the train.

Contemporary photographs show that some of the guests actually dined in their top hats! The epicurean meal was more than worthy of the occasion. The final gesture of the proceedings was the presentation by the Chairman of the Great Central to the Rt Hon C. T. Ritchie, President of the Board of Trade, of a large silver casket containing a vellum scroll with a plan of the Great Central route. In his speech Ritchie observed, quite rightly, that there was little probabilty that any further great trunk route would ever enter London. Sadly, Sir Edward Watkin had to attend the celebration in a bath chair and, indeed, had only two more years to live. After the dinner and speeches, the guests then proceeded to platform 2 where Ritchie and his wife, the Directors and Heads of Departments, all assembled on a dais.

Ritchie pulled a simple silver lever to admit steam into the cylinders of locomotive 861 and the train moved slowly out of Marylebone to the cheers of the assembled guests and the general public lining the route beyond. Services for the public were instituted on 15 March and the first three trains carried four, fourteen and thirty-four passengers respectively. These initial figures were, unfortunately, all too significant, since the low density of traffic underlined the competition that the line was to face from the other major established companies with routes into London.

Nottingham Joint was now complete and the station was ready to be opened. There was equal publicity from both companies but, not surprisingly, the choice of name for the station was the cause of disagreement. The Great Central naturally wanted to adopt the name 'Central' but the Northern was outraged and gave out tickets with 'Joint' stamped on them. On 24 May 1900 (Queen Victoria's birthday) the first train from Manchester bound for Marylebone drew into the station. The town clerk, realising the significance of the date, put forward his inspired proposal to name the station 'Victoria'.

Commemorative medallions were struck by a Nottingham firm to celebrate the event. Although the station no longer exists, the modern shopping mall which occupies the site perpetuates the original name.

The opening of the Great Central, however, was not without problems. South of Quainton Road, the Metropolitan, under Bell, owned the railway and became hostile to Watkin, who no longer held a position of authority in the Company. As a result of this feud a further section (No. 12) was authorised so that the GC could provide a link with the Great Western. It was decided that the connection at Aylesbury was unsuitable, so a link was built between Woodford and Banbury and opened about the time that Woodford South curve fell into disuse. An alliance was formed with the GW but the estimated cost of the link was £300,000 and

Marylebone departure
No. 427, *City of London*, is seen here leaving Marylebone on a Manchester working.

the MS&L could not afford this. The GW provided the capital, having broken its agreement with the Midland which stated that they would encourage rivals. The MS&L were to be responsible for the construction and actual operation of the link. By the end of July 1897 Walter Scott & Co were chosen as contractors and promised

completion of the project within two years. The line left the London Extension near Culworth and joined the GW north-east of the station at Banbury. The layout provided double track and later intermediate halts at Eydon Road and Chalcome Road were provided. By 1 June 1900 goods and mineral trains had begun to

Marylebone
On the left, underneath the large building, where the tank wagons are, was the milk dock. The carriages below, a set of Gresley articulated suburban stock standing on the outer stabling siding of platform 1, were used for local workings. The tracks either side of the roadway to the right of the coach stabling siding lead into platforms 1 and 2 respectively.

use this section and thereafter Great Central freight for the GW was no longer exchanged at Aylesbury. Passenger services ran from August of that year, two per day from Leicester to Oxford, supplemented by three trains shuttling between Woodford and Banbury. The benefits of the line were soon apparent from the volume of traffic.

Meanwhile the GW was searching for a shorter route to Paddington and soon found an obvious solution to their problem. They decided to improve the line from Old Oak Common to High Wycombe and to improve the Wycombe Railway through Princes Risborough to Aylesbury. Although Parliament approved these plans, the Great Central stepped in because it saw an opportunity of extracting itself from Bell's clutches. They planned to link Neasden and Northolt. The Metropolitan company was outraged but, in spite of this, the Great Central was provoked into taking action to prevent any further needless obstruction, delays and expense. The Great Central was quick to realise that herein lay an oppor-

tunity of stealing the limelight and of participating in the Birmingham venture. On 12 August 1898 the Neasdon-Northolt line Act was passed. Bell, however, continued to make transactions impossible for the Great Central even though he had granted a licence for running rights over Metropolitan metals. The Great Central had no option but to resort to litigation. In 1898 the GC and GW began to plan the new route to London. The two companies formed a joint

Marylebone looking northwards *Top*
An unusual picture showing the vast old goods yard in the raised area on the left, which is now a GLC housing estate. The track in the foreground has also been much reduced as traffic demand has diminished.

Marylebone *Bottom*
Tank No. 449 leaves the throat of Marylebone with a 'down' local train for Woodford Halse.

43

Marylebone right away!
With a massive burst of steam B16 61438, in immaculately lined black livery, sets out on a Nottingham working. The little metal structure above the front coach is part of the mechanical coaling plant.

Aylesbury station
Junction for Princes Risborough, the station was served by a wide variety of services from the GW, GC and Metropolitan Railways. The goods shed behind the footbridge is typical of the GW design and there seems to be a fair amount of activity on the London platform. The man with the oil can and urn, between the two tracks, suggests that a train is due.

committee to construct a line from Northolt to Wycombe and to improve the line beyond. The former Wycombe Railway was purchased and the Great Central was to build a line through to Grendon Underwood – a junction formed near the Metropolitan's Quainton station. The layout allowed for double track, with quadruple track at stations, the latter being built with tracks through instead of around. There were other consequential requirements: it would have to connect with the Maidenhead branch and Aylesbury, and provide a suitable interchange at Princes Risborough for the Oxford and Watlington branches and, of course, join up with the London Extension. As this route was 4½ miles longer than that of the Metropolitan, it was important to have the least possible gradients and least curvature to facilitate high-speed running, which would compensate for the extra mileage. In this the Great Central would have the advantage since the Metropolitan was, at the best of times, highly congested and a poor route in respect of speed.

Construction work began in 1901 at a cost of £299,000. Thomas Oliver & Sons (Rugby) were responsible for the Neasden to Northolt section and Messrs Pattinsons (of Westminster) contracted to supply three stations at Wembley Hill, South Harrow, and Sudbury & Harrow Road, at a cost of £12,000. Saxby & Farmer received the signalling contract at £5,915. Fortunately there were few problems apart from the massive retaining wall necessary at Wembley, a fly-under connection with Northolt main line and a short tunnel (203 yards long) at South Harrow under the District railway. Near Wembley Hill (now the Wembley Complex), Watkin had planned to erect a sort of 'Eiffel' tower, some 800 feet high, in the park which was part of his estate. The actual structure never got beyond the first stage and even this no longer survives.

Meanwhile, in the Metropolitan camp various changes were occurring which led to an improvement in relations with the Great Central. This situation was mainly due to the resignation of Bell through ill health, and the appointments of

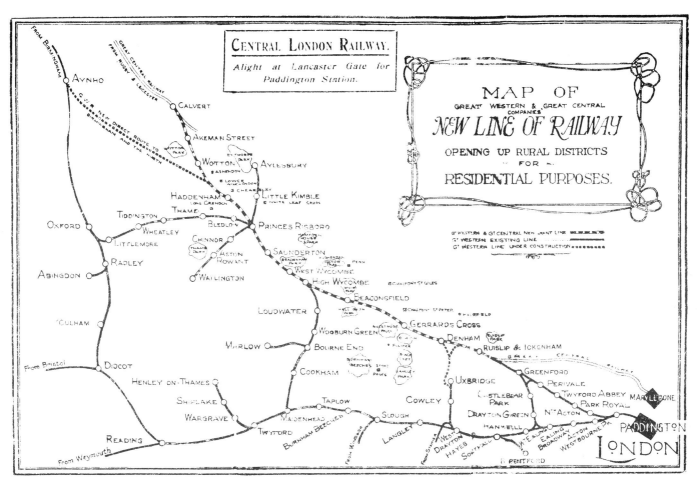

Neasden
Engine No. 81 of the Metropolitan 'E'
class and No. 95 *Robert H. Selbie* stand at
Neasden metropolitan motive power depot
in 1931.

Neasden North Box
Repairing the permanent way is one of the
more important tasks of a railway company
and here two men are seen ballasting the
line. In the background, amidst the various
arrays of signals, is the Great Central's
Neasden depot.

Charles Ellis as General Manager and Colonel Mellor as Chairman. Furthermore, the Metropolitan had just completed the widening of the line from Canfield to Harrow South Junction but this was small consolation for Watkin, who died on 13 April 1901 at Rose Hill in Northenden, Cheshire, aged 82. The new Chairman was Sir Sam Fay, born a Hamble-le-Frith in December 1856. A Huguenot by descent, Fay was the second son of a farmer. Educated at Fareham, he joined the London and South Western Railway, working then at Itchen Abbas. After promotions in the LSWR and a move to the Midland and South Western

Junction, he went to the GCR.

Even though Sir Sam Fay had cemented a firm friendship with the Metropolitan, the contracts for the GW and GC route were landed. Pauling & Co were awarded the High Wycombe-Northolt contract (£580,000) and MacKay & Davis that for the remodelling work (£116,797). Louis Nott was responsible for the Princes Risborough-Grendon Underwood line (£170,276), extended to Ashenden, the point of departure for the GW line to Aynho. The headquarters of the southern section was at Gerrards Cross and the complex there included offices, workshops, stables and an engine shed for 22

Wembley
Watkins Tower, as seen from the Neasden area where the Great Central met the Metropolitan Railway.

Wonderful Wembley
The massive tower in the background was part of a scheme by Edward Watkin, similar to that of the Eiffel Tower. However, due to lack of finance the tower never went beyond the first stage and was later demolished. The main line is in the foreground and it is just possible to make out Wembley Hill station in the background which was designed to serve the park.

Denham
On a fine day '8B' No. 267 works a 'down' Manchester express which would have travelled up to the main part of the London Extension by utilising the link from Ashendon to Grendon Underwood Junction. Denham was known for its connections with the film industry, set up there in 1936 on a 28-acre site according to the dream of Sir Alexander Corda. It was not unknown for expresses to stop at Denham on special occasions and in 1922 a Grand National race train was advertised and it was possible to have lunch and dinner on the train as well as' go to the races for a First Class fare of £3.5s. (£3.25p).

locomotives. Work began early in 1901. The mileposts ran from zero (Northolt) whereas on the Great Central, zero was Manchester London Road. The line crossed the Ealing Ruislip road by an unusual girder bridge, the Uxbridge branch of the Metropolitan south of Ruislip and, finally, the Grand Union canal by a viaduct (198 yards long) and the river Colne by a viaduct (250 yards long). Other viaducts were those between Denham and Gerrards Cross over the river Misbourne (5 spans) and at Chalfont Road (5 spans). Between Gerrards Cross and High Wycombe there were extensive cuttings, embankments and a tunnel at White House Farm (347 yards long) – the latter being the scene of an accident in which six men lost their lives owing to a fall of earth – and finally a viaduct (3 spans). The building of a new station at High Wycombe with staggered platforms needed no less than 1¼ million Stafford blue engineering bricks, a hallmark of Great Central constructions. In addition, goods and engine sheds were provided and the track at High Wycombe was doubled: the new goods yard accommodated approximately 200 wagons. Between Saunderton and Princes Risborough an interesting feature

was a deep cutting through chalk. Saunderton station was modernised and a new one built at Princes Risborough. Stations were planned to include side platforms and loops off the running lines (except at West Wycombe, Saunderton and Akeman Street). The loops at Gerrards Cross and Beaconsfield could hold a train of 80 wagons (727 yards long). From Ruislip to Haddenham, the stations were of the GW pattern. Likewise the signalling and permanent way followed the pattern set by the GWR.

Beyond Ashendon, however, the GCR pattern was followed. The line was open to goods traffic from 20 November 1905. In April of the following year suburban passenger services were inaugurated. The total cost of the line had been £40,000 a mile. Henderson, toasting the venture at a public celebration at High Wycombe, pointed out the undoubted potentiality of this as a direct link with the West of England and with the Midlands. Next a short branch from the GW and GC to Uxbridge (High Street station) was constructed and the GC incorporated the GW line from Princes Risborough to Aylesbury. Finally, in 1908, Northolt junction was opened and likewise the GW Ashenden-Aynho line. Two further

Princes Risborough
One of the more splendid Newton collection pictures is this one which shows the full extent of the station, trackwork, signals and cabin. The station was the junction for Chinnor, Aylesbury and Oxford, while the main line ran through to Birmingham. The signal cabin, which has a frame the length of a cricket pitch, and the lower quadrant signals have a distinct Great Western flavour.

On the Wycombe line
B7 No. 547, passing South Ruislip on an express. The B7s, or 'Black Pigs' as they were known, were not usually seen on London Extension trains and were noted for their reduced domes, cabs and chimneys which enabled them to work on other parts of the LNER System.

High Wycombe
The rebuilding of the line through High Wycombe necessitated the building of a new 'up' line platform, as there was not enough space to accommodate the four lines in the old station area and a platform as well. Access to the new 'up' platform was made via the subway depicted.

Denham Golf Club
Originally opened as a platform in 1912, Denham Golf Club became a halt. Apart from the golf course there was little else in the area to attract revenue until a development company announced plans for a miniature town on the site of an old army camp. This winter 1984 shot shows that the station has retained much of its original character with the GWR pagoda-style shelter, etc.

Aylesbury station
F1 5594 stands at platform 2 of Aylesbury station with a local passenger working from Quainton Road in 1929. The station buildings have changed very little since this picture was taken, although Aylesbury has only a minor role as a railway terminus.

West Wycombe
Taken around 1905, this picture shows the finishing touches being put to the station. This station was put in for two purposes, namely to serve West Wycombe park and to cater, in the long run, for the expansion of High Wycombe. At this stage only the centre roads had to be installed before trains could run. West Wycombe, however, was an early casualty of closure in 1958 as it succumbed to the strong competition from the fast bus service in the race to attract local passengers.

stations were added at Denham Golf Club and Seer Green (formerly Beaconsfield Golf Links).

Changes were also being effected on the Metropolitan section in 1904 with the purchase of running rights by the Great Central, which had formed a joint committee named the Metropolitan and Great Central Joint Committee. The latter took over the 51¾ miles of track mainly in Buckinghamshire:

	Miles
Harrow South-Harrow	¼
Harrow-Rickmansworth	8
Rickmansworth-Chalfont	4⅜
Chalfont-Chesham	4
Chalfont-Aylesbury	16⅜
Aylesbury-Verney	12⅜
Brill branch	6⅜

The transfer fee and rental amounted to a sum of £165,500, with an annual payment of £44,000 to the Metropolitan. By 1906 it was possible for the GC to begin a new suburban service from Marylebone-Amersham-Aylesbury. The Metropolitan had been built in stages, with the first length to Harrow opened in 1880, followed by Pinner in 1885, and Rickmansworth by 1887. The line from Chalfont to Chesham was completed in 1889.

From Chalfont Road to Aylesbury the construction took the longest time: authorised in 1881 it was not completed until 1892. In fact Aylesbury station was nearer Stoke Mandeville than its own town. Aylesbury to Verney Junction and the Brill branch lines had already been established. The latter, like the route to Chesham, was a single track line. Between Aylesbury and Verney the line passed through the estates of the Duke of Buckingham and of Sir Harry Verney, connecting with the GWR and London and North Western Railway at either end. The Duke was Chairman, with Sir Harry Verney acting as deputy Chairman. The Duke recognised that it would be important to take the line near his house at Wotton, and this had influenced the choice of route. The Aylesbury & Buckingham Railway, as it was named, had four intermediate stations at Waddesdon (for the use of Baron de Rothschild who lived at Waddesdon Manor), Quainton, Granborough Road and Winslow Road.

Quainton was also the starting point for another line before the arrival of the London Extension, namely the Wotton Tramway, con-

Uxbridge
'Pull In', says the sign outside the old GWR terminus at the bottom of Uxbridge High Street in this September 1929 picture. The Oxford Road ran past the station and already the railway was feeling the effects of road competition. When the station opened in May 1907, there were girders right across the road in anticipation of the line being taken round the outskirts of the town with the Vine Street station. Uxbridge was so proud of its new link in 1907 that Lucy and Birch, the local printers, produced a commemorative postcard. The first station-master was a Mr Carpenter who had originally been at Hungerford. In 1922 the bridge over High Street was removed and whilst the girders were being winched down, some of the workmen nearly became entangled with the chains.

Granborough Road
F7 motor train 8307 stands at Granborough Road on the Verney Junction–Aylesbury run. The station, similar in design to Quainton and Winslow Road, succumbed to closure after a very short existence.

struction of which commenced in September 1870. By March 1871 wagons were drawn along this by horses. The line formally opened in April as far as Wotton and reached Church Siding (a 1½-mile branch) by November and the terminus, at Brill hill, by the summer of 1872. There were two small spurs, one to the gasworks for Waddesdon Manor, the other to a brickworks at Brill, serving this local industry.

There were five stations, Waddesdon, Westcott, Wotton, Church Siding and Wood Siding. Many commodities were carried over this line, particularly agricultural freight and felled timber; passenger traffic, however, gave a poor return. The rolling stock consisted of two 8hp Aveling and Porter geared engines and an antiquated coach. The engines travelled at 4mph.

1894 saw a change of identity for the Wotton Tramway and Wescott became Westcott: the Tramway came under the control of the Oxford & Aylesbury Tramroad Company who improved the track by relaying it with 50lb flat-bottomed rails and added a new locomotive to the stock. The

O&AT also proposed to extend the line to Oxford (an additional 11 miles of track) but this plan was never carried into effect since the line was absorbed by the Metropolitan in 1899 and subsequently by the Metropolitan and GC Joint Committee in 1906.

Between Harrow-on-the-Hill and Aylesbury there were stations at Pinner, Northwood, Rickmansworth, Chorley Wood, Chalfont Road (renamed Chalfont & Latimer in November 1951), Amersham, Great Missenden, Wendover and Stoke Mandeville. Two new stations were opened at Sandy Lodge and North Harrow in 1910 and 1915 respectively.

1905 saw the beginning of an electrified service to Harrow-on-the-Hill and Uxbridge. The latter station was completely reconstructed and resignalled for the new service. At Aylesbury, however, moves had been made to remodel the station and to remove the treacherous south curve (which had claimed the life of an engine driver and fireman). This involved the construction of two new signal boxes north and south of the station. The work cost £9,000 and was completed in 1908.

Quainton Road
Manning Wardle 0-6-0 ST at Quainton Road. After the sale of the geared loco these tanks became popular on the Wotton tramway with Wotton No. 1 previously named *Huddersfield*, Brill No. 2, and later Wotton No. 2, forming the workhorses of the line. Wotton No. 2 replaced *Huddersfield*.

Wotton Tramway & Great Central
These two stations were run by the same stationmaster and here Wotton Great Central is seen under construction and, like the rest of the stations on the Great Central avoiding line, Wotton was provided with loops and lavish goods facilities.

Wotton station
As well as the main-line station the Great Central also had running rights over the Wotton tramway. This picture shows Wotton station and the goods shed. The track was relaid in 1894 with flat-bottomed steel rails and to standard gauge.

Wotton tramway
One of the more bizarre locos was this Aveling and Porter 0-4-0 geared engine. Two of these worked the line and in appearance they were really no more than general traction engines, complete with flywheels, but fitted with flanged wheels.

Dutchlands summit
L1, 67751 with an 'up' local train from Aylesbury, consisting of eight Dreadnought coaches, wending its way towards Great Missenden station on a summer day in 1951.

Travel in style
One of the more interesting services offered by the Metropolitan was the Verney Junction Pullman, pictured at Chorley Wood in 1934. The pullmans were introduced during the war between the Metropolitan and Great Central Railways to compete for traffic beyond Harrow-on-the-Hill. The train was usually electrically-hauled and contained either one of the two pullman named *Mayflower* and *Galatea*. The two cars were finally withdrawn shortly after the outbreak of the Second World War.

Opposite
46112, 'Royal Scot' Class *Sherwood Forester* is seen here passing Amersham on a Marylebone to Nottingham working in 1963.

Sherwood Forester

FORWARD.

Annesley

At this lonely spot on the line from Sheffield a junction was installed which heralded the commencement of the London Extension, the last main line to London. In this picture, looking north towards Sheffield in 1896, a contractor's loco is seen standing on the 'up' main with an engineering train carrying materials for works further down the line. The course of the 'down' line is ready for track-laying and marked out with a dotted line on the picture.

Chapter Three

SHERWOOD FORESTER NOTTINGHAM TO LEICESTER

It was between the years 1910 and 1914 that the Great Central reached a climax in its growth; the last extensions and new lines had already been completed or were about to be completed. It was due to the efforts of two men that the GC actually began to appear as a more efficient and concentrated enterprise, and they were Sir Sam Fay and his chief locomotive and rolling stock engineer, John G. Robinson, who had begun his career serving an apprenticeship at Swindon from whence he went on to become assistant locomotive superintendent of the Waterford and Limerick and Western Railway. He joined the Great Central in May 1900 and was appointed locomotive, carriage and wagon chief and later chief mechanical engineer. Because he originated from a railway background, he met the challenge of his new job on the Great Central admirably and remained in the post until grouping in 1923 when, due to his outstanding ability, he was offered the chance to take charge of Motive Power for the London North Eastern. However, by this time Robinson was an old man and so he made the way clear for Nigel Gresley of the Great Northern.

During the Robinson regime no fewer than twenty-seven different types of locomotive were introduced, though not all were destined for the London Extension but, judging by the designs which did appear, it is easy to see that the line was mainly designed for goods and mineral traffic. This fact is borne out by Robinson's first Class, the J11s, which were primarily known as goods engines although they did see some passenger service. These engines affectionately known as 'Pom Poms' were the pioneers of Robinson's programme to build, rebuild and improve existing locomotives like the Sacré engines for long-haul through trains. The first type to appear on these duties were the 'Atlantics' which remained commonplace until the late 1930s between Marylebone and Nottingham. By 1913, with the advent of the 'Director' class some of the 'Atlantics' began to be displaced from the London Extension, as the Directors took on the London-Manchester and other long-haul trains but they were not shedded on the London Extension until after the Second World War. Apart from these two

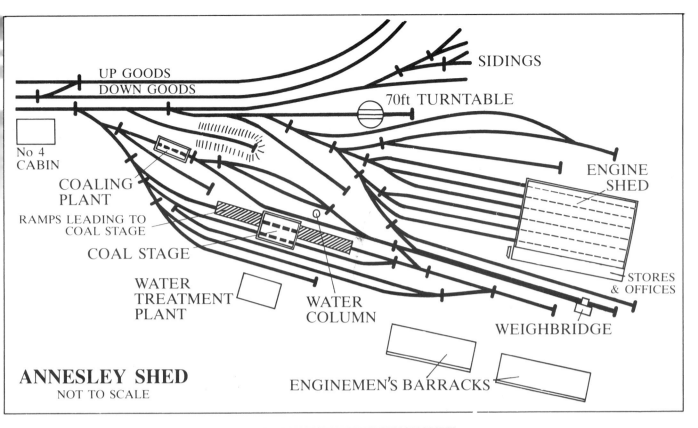

ANNESLEY SHED
NOT TO SCALE

(Diagram labels: UP GOODS, DOWN GOODS, SIDINGS, 70ft TURNTABLE, ENGINE SHED, No 4 CABIN, COALING PLANT, RAMPS LEADING TO COAL STAGE, COAL STAGE, STORES & OFFICES, WATER TREATMENT PLANT, WATER COLUMN, WEIGHBRIDGE, ENGINEMEN'S BARRACKS)

Annesley
Looking south in the same year the 'up' line of the London Extension is in place, while the 'down' line and connection to the Sheffield routes have yet to be installed. Note the massive amount of earth that has been removed from the existing embankment by Logan & Hemmingway.

classes, several other Robinson designs saw service on the London Extension such as the D9s, B7s, B3s, L1s, D11s and D10s.
For local services Robinson and the Great Central works outshopped tanks known as the 'Coronation Tanks' owing to the national event which took place in the year they first appeared (1911). As well as these there were the 9L bunker engines which provided a stalwart selection of local services. Other favourites on the Great Central were the N5 tanks which performed a varied selection of duties. Indeed it was with these designs that the great 'John G' was able to boost the new railway which already had strong competition.

Sir Sam Fay's part in the campaign, however, was to promote the line and this he achieved by a series of slogans which were dreamed up by his publicity committee. Fay was very cunning and appointed an artist, named W. J. Stuart, to manage his promotions. Stuart, by his profession, realised

Hucknall Central

The station, looking northwards towards Annesley in 1952. Hucknall was served by three stations and the Central station was the least convenient for the town in true GC fashion. Most of its trade came from local workers boarding the Dido train to Annesley works. Indeed, after a rather chequered career Hucknall Central closed in 1963 with the withdrawal of local services.

Bulwell Common *Bottom*

On a greyish day in March 1952 4-6-0 No. 61063 is seen leaving the island platform at Bulwell Common with the Annesley *Dido* whose name is said to have originated from a rather dubious connection between Queen Dido of Carthage, Nestead Abbbey and a corruption into railway parlance of nearby Diadem Hill. Another theory was that Queen Victoria was being compared to Queen Dido in some way. Whereas the actual origin of the name *Dido* comes simply from an abbreviation of 'Day In Day Out', because the train ran frequently to and from Annesley depot. A Royal Navy cruiser on the Clyde was to be named 'Dido' in honour of Queen Victoria but its timber supports under the hull collapsed while it was being built and it was not launched according to plan.

that it was necessary to capture every spare space for posting Great Central propaganda. Posters appeared in kiosks, trains, shop windows, and on hoardings giving details of train times and destinations. Notices of football matches also carried the same information. Such slogans as 'Rapid travel in luxury' and 'Live in the country' became household words. The Great Central also laid on special trains for cup finals and on one poster of the Manchester City v Bolton Wanderers match in 1904 it actually showed the winning goal, which by a strange coincidence happened in the way depicted. Other special workings included holiday expresses and inter-regional trains, which all helped to build the image of the railway.

Unfortunately, a temporary set-back was experienced by the Great Central in 1911, caused by the first national strike of railway-men, who were not content with the conditions under which they

Bagthorpe Junction
On a fine summer Saturday in 1957, J39 No. 64976 eases its way over Bulwell viaduct with a Sheffield Nottingham train which would have called at all stations en route. The rolling stock which was in the post nationalisation blood and custard livery consists of a mixture of Gresley and British Rail designs. Note also the train is carrying a parcels van. In the foreground are the telegraph wires for the Midland line while behind the buildings on the right hand side ran the River Leen. Out of sight behind the train lay Bulwell lane factory.

Bagthorpe Junction
Climbing out of Bulwell common station which lay beyond the road overbridge in the background Class V2 2-6-2 60867 makes light work of its train of mineral empties which were probably bound for Hucknall Colliery. On the right lay the former Leen Valley Branch. This line passed under the embankment which carried the GC main line before joining up with the chord from the GC up main line to the Leen valley line.

worked. Finally, after a long and hard period of bargaining the strike came to an end with the Great Central employees achieving their aim; the increased expenditure for improving the conditions was approved in 1911. Sir Sam Fay had taken an important part in the negotiations and is reputed to have said during the strike that he would be as ready to shake hands with a labour leader as with a duke, but he preferred not to live with either. Around this time three new halts were provided on the London Extension, at Rushcliffe near East Leake, Chalcombe Road and Eydon Road on the Banbury-Woodford Halse line. The latter two halts were built of wood and were opened on 17 April 1911 and 1 October 1917 respectively.

There was a steady expansion of passenger traffic, services and facilities. Services included excursions to the Isle of Man, Bangor and Menai. These trains operated on Mondays, Tuesdays, Fridays and Saturdays, leaving Sheffield at 7.30 am and arriving at Liverpool at 9.40 am to connect with the

steamers. In 1911 a breakfast car express service was instituted between Sheffield and Marylebone, calling at Chesterfield and Nottingham and Leicester. The journey time of just under two hours compares very favourably with the current Inter-City timings for the Sheffield-London run. By 1914 most of the modern locomotives and carriages had been introduced together with twenty restaurant cars. These were used in holiday trains which started in June and helped to support the growth of the leisure movement. The full programme began on 13 July with through trains to Blackpool, Aberystwyth, Ilfracombe, Skegness and Scarborough. Workings of this type continued right up until the demise of the London Extension.

The main centres on the London Extension were Nottingham and Leicester.

The city of Nottingham, situated on the rivers Trent and Leen, dates back to AD922, when it was fortified by Edward the Elder. A castle was erected later by the Normans

Bagthorpe Junction
A4 Streamlined Pacifics and Pullman cars were a rarity on Great Central metals and here No. 60014 Silver Link on an Ian Allan Trains Illustrated excursion is seen pounding through Bulwell Common Island platform with a mixed rake of Pullmans and BR Mark 1 stock. This train had probably originated from Kings Cross due to the 34A Shedplate on the front of the loco.

Bagthorpe Junction

The Annesley Dido stands amid a cloud of steam at Bulwell Common waiting to pick up railwaymen bound for Annesley depot. At the head of the train is a Class N7 0-6-2 which is drawing two ex G.C. coaches. Of interest is the intricate pointwork in the foreground which gave access to the exchange sidings which held traffic for the Leen Valley line for the most part.

New Basford

'Royal Scot' Class 46165 *The Ranger (12th London Regiment)* leaving the carriage shed sidings and ambling through the station with empty stock for Nottingham Victoria in June 1964. Basford was the last station before the start of the long complex of tunnels which began at Sherwood Rise. The station also boasted a large goods yard with a substantial handling shed which still stands today. The carriage sidings and large goods depot were provided here and at Wilford, to the south of Nottingham, as there was only enough space for the station on the Victoria site. The service was mainly used in morning and evening periods by hosiery and engineering workers who travelled on the route to Derby Friargate via Ilkeston.

New Basford

A fairly smart looking B1 4-6-0 No. 61390
is seen here at New Basford with a train of
empty stock for the carriage sheds which
are to the left of the picture. The carriages
had probably formed a Marylebone to
Nottingham express. In the background
one can just make out the canopy and
buildings of the small island platform at
New Basford. Also note the hill on the
horizon through which the Great Central
had to bore a tunnel (Sherwood Rise)
whose northern portal lay at the entrance
to Basford Goods yard.

New Basford

'Ivatt' Class 4 43091 simmers gently as it
backs away from the carriage sidings in
June 1964, also towards Nottingham
Victoria. The sheds and carriage storage
roads became less and less used when
services were withdrawn from Victoria. In
the background is the large goods handling
shed which continued to be used well after
the station closed.

under William I, but the castle was destroyed in 1651 during the civil war and not rebuilt until 1679. The castle and the surrounding area is still one of the finest parts of Nottingham today. Under the castle lie a series of caves which go to make up Mortimer's Hole, which was used as a secret entrance to the fortress to arrest Roger Mortimer, the Earl of March, who was later hanged at Tyburn, London. Many other such workings appear in Nottingham's easily-worked sandstone, as it was as cheap to tunnel as to build above ground. Apart from the castle and the caves, Nottingham boasts a fine selection of elegant buildings, beautiful parks and boulevards, upholding the comment once made to me that Nottingham was the pride of the Midlands. Careful planning over the years has ensured that the city's heritage has not been despoiled. One of the oldest buildings in Nottingham is The Trip to Jerusalem Inn, which is noted for its locally brewed beer and, dating back to 1189, it claims to be the oldest inn in the country. Nearby is another old building which houses the Lace Centre which was one of the chief local industries along with coal mining, hosiery, cycle works, engineering, tobacco and pharmaceuticals. This was one of the prime reasons for railways arriving in the Nottingham area and the Great Central hoped to be able to cash in on the growth of industry. The Great Central established a goods depot near Wilford Road and three passenger stations at Arkwright Street, Victoria and Carrington. The first of these, Arkwright Street, was the final outpost of the line in Nottingham, lasting until 1969 when it ceased to role as the Northern terminus of the GC truncated commuter service. The name of the station originated from the name of Richard Arkwright who invented the spinning frame. Another famous name in Nottingham was Jesse Boot of Boots the chemists, and it was he who created a large part of the university.

Returning to the railway, Victoria didn't gain its name until 1900, when the name was changed from Central to Victoria in honour of the Queen. The station itself sat in a large well and it was possible to take the train for a variety of destinations. Above ground there was the hotel, which provided a resting place for weary travellers; this still stands although no longer a transport hotel but one catering for scores of Nottingham's tourists who come to enjoy the shopping, entertainments, monuments and the Robin Hood legend. Victoria station was rased to the ground as soon as it was closed and two temporary lines were laid through its site for the conveyance of freight. However, they were soon removed as

Carrington
Taken in November 1984 the booking hall and station house at Carrington Station have now found another use and the shop still boasts the name Carrington station newsagents. Carrington was one of the three non island platforms on the London Extension, situated in the cutting between Mansfield Road and Sherwood Rise tunnels. It was never a well used station and fell victim to closure in LNER days. Its busiest time was probably when it was used as a relief terminus along with Arkwright Street while Victoria was being completed in 1899-1900.

Carrington
In this 1966 view a number of changes are evident. The station has been closed for forty-odd years and the London Extension trunk service has finished a month previously. Both the footbridge and crossover have been taken out and one of the platform edges has been removed, while the other is in remarkably good condition considering how long it has been out of use. Note the 'Sulzer' (BR Class 25/1) which is stopped at the colour light signal just under the northern portal of Mansfield Road tunnel.

Nottingham Victoria
B5 6071 at the head of a South Wales express, standing at the south end of Nottingham Victoria with the 1.55pm departure on 29 June 1937. The stock is Great Western as, once it left the GC metals at Banbury, this train travelled over GWR territory down the Banbury and Cheltenham Railway and then to Swansea.

Nottingham Victoria
5437 *Prince George* seen here on pilot duty
on 19 July 1937 stands on the central road
with a group of early Gresley coaches. This
road berthed the rolling stock of arriving
local trains.

Nottingham Victoria   *Left*
An unidentified class 04 GCR 2-8-0 typical
of the Robinson style of locomotives. They
were known for their low maintenance
costs and had long lives as most 8-coupled
engines, and saw service on both passenger
and goods workings. They were also known
for their stalwart performances during
both world wars and were referred to as
'Engines that won the war'. Here one of
the engines is thundering through Victoria
with an 'up' coal.

Nottingham Victoria   *Right*
LNER 5363 on a northbound Marylebone–
Manchester express with a rake of Gresley
stock on 13 May 1934, entering the south
end of Mansfield Road tunnel. On the
right, behind the train, is Nottingham No.
4 signal box, while on the left of the tunnel
mouth is the turntable.

Nottingham Victoria
'Footballer' 2853 *Huddersfield Town* at
platform 4 with an 'up' train. The coach
behind the engine is a GCR 'Barnum'
vehicle and carries a carriage destination
board. Note the sleek streamlining of the
engine.

Nottingham Victoria

4-4-0 30925 *Cheltenham* pilots 2p 4-4-0
40646 waiting to leave on a Railway
Correspondance & Travel Society 'East
Midlander' bound for Darlington and
York on 13 May 1962. These trips were
very popular and several were run in the
final years of the line. The engine 40546
had been officially condemned two days
previous to the trip. Note the clocktower
above the engines and the bridge which
was added after the construction of the
main station.

Great Central Railway, ex-MS&LR 0-6-2T
No. 773 at Nottingham Victoria, 27 May
1901.

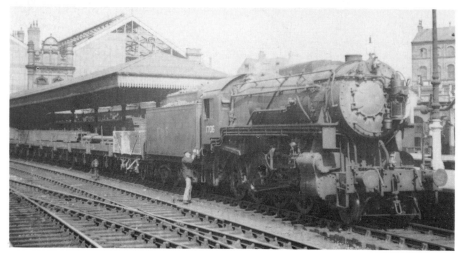

Nottingham Victoria

The date is 1943 in the midst of the Second
World War and a plumber's delight sits at
platform 7 in the form of American 2-8-0
1706 on an 'up' goods, carrying mainly
steel girders and rolls. The driver is about
to board the engine and set off on this
sunny day.

Nottingham Victoria
4-4-0 2654 *Walter Burgh Gair* leaves on a stopping train for Leicester Central on 23 June 1949, pulling a rake of Gresley stock out of the station under Parliament Street and the south signal cabin, before entering Thurland Street tunnel which emerged at Weekday Cross.

Nottingham Victoria
LNER (ex GCR) 4-4-2T 6065 C13 tank stands at the south end of the station looking towards Parliament Street. The C13s, or 9K Class, had been allocated to the Marylebone local services but were transferred to the more remote parts of the Great Central at grouping, making this appearance somewhat unusual.

North and line-up
Wrong line running at 'The Vic' *c* 1933 with 2842 *Kilverstone Hall* on a 'down' express waiting for the right of way. 2842 is standing in the southbound platform due to trackwork on the other side of the station. In the bay platform another engine gets up steam, to take out a local, probably to Sheffield, while yet another train in platform 10 (the outer one on the island) eagerly awaits passengers.

Nottingham *Top*
Noted for its fine ales, Nottingham also boasts the oldest pub in England, known as the Trip To Jerusalem which was built in the thirteenth century. The public house is situated in the Brewhouse yard and still boasts a fair selection of home brewed ales.

Nottingham *Top right*
Victoria Station and Hotel (from Mansfield Road) which fitted gracefully into the rest of the street. Today only the clocktower remains of this once splendid edifice.

The Castle *Centre*
Nottingham Castle in its present form was built by the Dukes of Newcastle in the 17th Century on the site of the Medieval royal castle. It is now a museum and houses a fine collection of ceramics, silver, glass, carvings, historical displays as well as containing a fine selection of militaria mainly of the Sherwood Foresters regiment. Housing an art gallery displaying works of local painters the castle is probably one of the most prominent sites culturally and physically for it stands on a rock commanding a fine view of Nottingham.

A busy day at 'the Vic'
As workmen assemble for the busy day ahead one of the 106 LMS shunters, No. 12049 in BR days, which was based at Annesley, is seen here emerging from the southern end of Mansfield Road tunnel with a track train stacked with sections ready for laying. The date is 27 July 1957.

Weekday Cross

A rather delightful view of the rooftops of Fletchergate and Garners Hill. The dome in the top left-hand corner of the picture is that of the Town Hall, or 'Council House' as it is more affectionately known by the locals. The line to the right led off towards Colwick and Grantham, while that to the left led to London's Marylebone station. Here B1 4-6-0 61159 is seen on an 'up' 'South Yorkshireman' from Bradford on 10 May 1949.

Arkwright Street

At the opening of the line this was the terminus of the route until Victoria was completed and sixty-seven years later it was made the end of the line for the ill-fated commuter service implemented by British Railways in 1966, after the closure of the main route. Like Carrington, this was another non-island platform and here 9F 92096 is seen on an 'up' 'Windcutter' freight coasting through a deserted platform on 10 April 1965, two months before the cessation of freight.

Victoria bound

An immaculate B1 4-6-0 61390 in British Railways lined black livery simmers gently waiting to depart on an 'up' stopper, seen here at the Great Central's most southerly Nottingham station, Arkwright Street, on 15 May 1954 with three Thompson vehicles, stationed at Basford carriage shed. Note the marking 'Basford' on the front carriage.

Arkwright Street
Nottingham from the Town Arms, near Trent bridge: part of a panoramic view, which shows the area known as the Meadows.

Wilford Road
K3 2-6-0 61809 on a Manchester–Marylebone express passing over the river Trent and Nottingham Goods South box on 28 July 1951. Note the unusual arrangement of the signal gantry on the left, which was intended to give loco crews a clear view of the signal.

British Railways made other arrangements for the traffic. Construction of one of Nottingham's new shopping centres started in 1968: the Victoria Centre. Today it is only possible to view the clock tower and the southern portal of Mansfield Road tunnel through which once bustled trains to and from Manchester and Sheffield. At the north end of Mansfield Road tunnel lay Nottingham's third station, namely Carrington, which was the first casualty on the London Extension, closing in September 1928.

The following year the new Council House was opened in Market Square which is one of the most impressive buildings in Nottingham. One other building which commands interest is the Theatre Royal which was recently restored to all its Victorian splendour. Examples of outdoor leisure include a fine range of parks at Colwick, Woollaton, the University Park, the Embankment and Sherwood forest, and the Nottingham Goose Fair which is held in October and has been traditional since 1284.

Moving further down the line, the first station is Ruddington which served a rather small local community. Ruddington's real main-

Wilford Road
B1 4-6-0 61182 on an 'up' South Yorkshireman from Bradford, seen here passing Wilford Brick sidings on the right of the picture behind the gate. The date is 7 June 1951. Note the stacks of bricks on the weedridden platform whose sidings were controlled by the box on the left.

Wilford 'Windcutter'
9F 92071, on an Annesley–Woodford working, heads towards the brick sidings with little effort needed, as can be seen by the lack of steam, with a train of loaded coal wagons. The third wagon is carrying steel girders, while the fourth is a ventilated van with unknown cargo. The clean condition of the smokebox door shows clearly both number and shed plate 16D 'Annesley' home of the 9F Class.

Ruddington
C4 6088 on a local passenger working, seen here passing the goods yard. Meanwhile another engine is busy shunting wagons, one of which has obviously come from the London Brighton and South Coast line though it has not yet been repainted with Southern Region markings. The date is 1925, two years after the formation of the big four railway companies.

stay was freight for the Ministry of Defence depot which had its own railway complex which is now isolated from the main British Railways network. The station closed in 1963 as part of the rundown of local services but continued to be served by goods traffic until September 1983. However, one final visit was made on 9 June 1984 with a special called the 'Ruddington Requiem'. Moving on through the fine Nottinghamshire countryside the next station is East Leake, situated in a deep cutting. The station served a small community like that at Ruddington, although the village has somewhat more character. One of the finest parts of East Leake is its church and the surrounding area has changed little since the time of the London Extension. Nearby is the quaint village of Gotham, which is noted for its gypsum works and this has provided freight traffic since 1895. The branch was authorised on 6 July of that year and it left the line two miles south of Ruddington. It was 2⅜ miles in length and single track, providing direct access to the gypsum beds, with a passing loop at J. W. Shepherd's plaster works.
    Before reaching Loughborough

Local industry
An early aerial view *c*1935, from above the area where Rushcliffe Halt was situated, shows one of the gypsum plants owned by Marbleegis Ltd Plaster Manufacturers. These buildings were served by sidings off the main line and a short branch was laid at Gotham to serve another gypsum works.

Ruddington village   *Opposite top*
The High Street *c*1910 showing a fairly busy scene at the local shops. The children in the foreground are probably on the way to school, while a horse and carriage wend their way up the hill.

Ruddington village   *Opposite bottom*
Church Street in 1910 with the school and the church in the background. A typical village scene with thatched cottages, gas lights and the odd 'local' standing in the street.

East Leake   *Centre*
'Thompson' B1 4-6-0 61028 *Umseke* seen here leaving East Leake on a Nottingham–Leicester stopping train on 25 September 1961, a year after the end of express working. Just visible at the Nottingham end of the station are the signal cabin and sidings which appear to be stabling a train of mineral wagons probably for the gypsum works at Gotham. Note the thick clump of fir trees which were planted when the line was built in order to camouflage the railway, a practice which occurred at many points along the route.

East Leake
The Great Central's last stand: a truncated and vastly modified diesel service. Here, a two-car diesel multiple unit arrives at the island platform, which is now no more than an unstaffed halt, with the 12.27pm ex Nottingham Arkwright Street, to Rugby Central. Note the indicator panel in the central part of the yellow warning strip.

East Leake

One of the quaint village streets showing some of the crooked-roofed cottages, built out of brick timber and thatch. In the background is St Mary's church. The East Leake area was known for its calcium sulphate deposits used in the manufacture of calcified plaster of paris.

East Leake

The peace and quiet of an East Leake street was typical of the areas that the Great Central Railway served. The houses in this 1948 picture are mainly of Edwardian and Victorian design.

Loughborough

5MT 44941 leaves Loughborough Central with a 'down' train to Nottingham Victoria just before closure. The date is June 1966 and the track is disappearing rapidly, with the goods yard and loops having been taken out. Both the water tower and station buildings miraculously survived until the Main Line Preservation Group moved in in 1969, shortly after the diesel service finished.

Loughborough
6906 *Chicheley Hall* on a Bournemouth–
Bradford express on 22 August 1964,
entering Loughborough Central from the
southern end. On summer Saturdays,
Great Western engines would work as far
as Leicester, and sometimes Nottingham,
from Banbury while a Great Central
Leicester engine would normally work the
train back. On these occasions it was not
unkown for Southern Region locomotives
and rolling stock to appear at Leicester
and Nottingham.

Loughborough Central
C4 'Atlantic' seen near Loughborough on
a 'down' Manchester express on 12 May
1927. The 'Atlantics' were stalwart
performers on the London Extension and
although they were used in the early years
of the line for light duties their ability to
take gradients at 60mph was outstanding,
while they could manage a downward trip
at up to 88mph. The LNER because of
their ability, built further members of the
Class and exploited them to the full on
more demanding workings. One of the
type's best performances was noted in July
1928 in *Railway Magazine* when No. 5361
covered the trip between Marylebone and
Leicester at an average speed of 65.7mph.

Loughborough
The market place, full of activity with
carts, stalls and people galore. The typical
wares that were sold at the market were
hosiery products, shoes and household
items.

Loughborough

5MT 'Stanier' 45334 crosses the Midland main line with a Nottingham–Marylebone semi-fast working on 1 August 1964. the leading vehicles are both ex LNER stock, the first being a Gresley BSK, while the second is of Thompson design. The bridge closest to the camera crosses the river Soar and spans four tracks. In the background, it is just possible to make out the platform and the short girder bridge over the freight lines of the St Pancras route. The vast complex of buildings belong to the Brush Engineering Works (now Hawker Siddeley).

Loughborough

Almost as if in mid-air, a rather grimy 9F 92372 heads south with a mixed goods, 1 August 1964.

Loughborough Central

D9 6038 charges along the bank towards Loughborough from Barnston tunnel with an 'up' express on 12 May 1927. The D9s were employed for the most part on passenger and were likened to being the passenger version of the J11 class. 40 engines in all were built between 1901 and 1904.

there was the small halt at Rushcliffe. As this was one of the newer stations along the line it was built according to the ordinary lay-out and not on the island principle. The first signs of the approach to Loughborough are the viaduct which crosses the river Soar and the outline of the Brush Electrical Engineering Works, now part of the Hawker Siddeley Group, which was established as the Falcon Works by Henry Hughes in 1865. The factory has been inherent in turning out trams, motor cars and diesel electric locomotives. Besides the Falcon Works, one of the oldest industries is the Taylor Bell Foundry, which has cast bells for

regular high-speed train service as well as a fair number of goods workings to and from the station yard. On the London Extension there was a passable service to London from Loughborough Central even in the early days. For example, in the summer of 1903 the Great Central offered five daytime trains through from Loughborough to London, and another five by changing at Leicester. From Loughborough to Manchester there were a total of five through and four connecting services. Local trains calling at stations between Leicester and Nottingham were frequent, amounting to approximately an

Loughborough
Taken around the time of the construction of the line, the picture shows the Town Hall with the clock at the top showing 5.25pm. Note the stage-set-like construction the building has, with a stone facade and brick surrounds. There is an unusually large gathering at the end of the street for this time of day; maybe it is market day.

St Pauls as well as for many instal-lations in Loughborough itself and throughout the county. Lough-borough is an old market town with a Grammar School dating back to 1495 and there is much evidence of hosiery manufacturing, just as in Nottingham and Leicester. Apart from hosiery there were brick-making, dyeworks and other general engineering industries. Loughborough's other claim to fame is that it created the first technical college which has now expanded to include other academic subjects.

Whilst Loughborough has expanded over the years, its rail-ways have seen some dramatic changes. The Midland line is still very much in evidence and sees a

hourly service. On top of this were the connecting services for the cross-country workings mentioned earlier in this chapter. Up to the time that the last part of the line closed, Loughborough Central boasted some kind of service and now, again, it is possible to see the station which has been restored to its original condition. To the north end of the station is the motive power depot which contains some fine examples of steam and diesel engines, some of whom worked on the Great Central main line to London. On weekends and bank holidays it is possible to enjoy 'A Return Trip to Yesterday' along the 5½ miles of preserved line to Rothley. Sadly, the line is now single track as the Great Central

Woodhouse Eaves Village
A beautiful scene overlooking the school and the sleepy little cottages of a typical Leicestershire village. Judging by the amount of smoke, the time of year is probably autumn; hardly smokeless fuel! The rambling fields and beautiful tree outlines provide a lovely backdrop. Note the rocky outcrop in the foreground.

Railway Society 1976 did not have sufficient funds to purchase the second track.

Leaving Loughborough on its journey to Quorn, the line passes houses on either side, with Charnwood Water not far in the distance which is a leisure and recreational area. The line then continues through the famous Quorn hunting country with the tiny hamlet of Woodthorpe visible in the distance. The line dips into a cutting in which lies a road overbridge carrying the access to the station at Quorn and Woodhouse, which is a fairly open

plan area with its large goods yard and country surroundings. The actual village of Quorn, or Quorndon as it is sometimes known, lies on one side of the line while Woodhouse lies on the other. Quorn, with its population of just over 3,000, is a traditional hunting village and the hounds of the famous Quorn Hunt take their name from the village. Worthy of special mention also is the church which has two unusual stone screens, and a fourteenth-century chapel full of memorials to the Farnham family; one of these was

Quorn & Woodhouse
On a dull afternoon during Easter weekend 1985, a train is just due to arrive at Quorn and Woodhouse from Rothley via the Swithland reservoir. Quorn and Woodhouse sees more life now as a station on part of the last main line to London than it did in the whole of its sixty-four years of existence. In the background is one of the original Great Central 'Barnum' saloons which took their name from transporting the Barnum and Bailey circus troup, here it is being used to house a static museum display of Railway Relics at the Great Central Railways, Quorn Easter Parade.

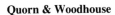

an Elizabethan gentleman who 'descended of an ancient with honours led his life' to the extent of winning a pension from his queen.

South of Quorn & Woodhouse, the railway passes through an area of outstanding beauty, through Buddon Wood, to the left of which lie the Mountsorrel granite quarries. At this point the line becomes viaduct-borne to cross the Swithland Reservoir from which can be obtained the best views of the surrounding area. The island in the centre is known as Brazil Island and the whole of the massive expanse of reservoir supplies the city of Leicester. When the line was built a gap was left for a station at Swithland but this never materialised, probably because it did not serve any centre. At this point also lay Swithland Sidings and a signal box to control the exchange facilities for the quarries at Mountsorrel.

Swinging away to the right, the line makes a short descent into the station at Rothley which forms the present terminus. Not far from the station lies the village of Rothley itself which has a population of approximately 4,000. One claim to fame exists, namely that Lord Macaulay was born at Rothley Temple, an Elizabethan house with a chapel that originally belonged to an affiliated order of the Knights Templar.

The final station before Leicester was Belgrave & Birstall, situated on the very outskirts of the city in a very deep cutting bounded by houses on both sides. Nearby is a golf course and this was one of the original reasons for the construction. As far as the prospects today are concerned the Great Central Railway 1976 intends to extend its operations to Belgrave and Birstall to the south and Ruddington to the north, to make a total of 17½ miles running distance.

Quorn & Woodhouse
Activities at the station today differ greatly from Watkin's time, as shown by the funfair, caravans and traction engines. In the midst of it all Class 40, No. 40 106 rumbles into the station with a fully-laden train of passengers on the return trip from Rothley. The engine is now named *Atlantic Conveyor* and bears an apt headboard 'The Green Goddess'.

Rothley
1083C C4 'Atlantic' works a train of six-wheeled stock on a Nottingham–Leicester local and is seen here at Rothley in 1923, the year of the beginning of the big four railway companies.

Rothley
A V2 60918 draws through Rothley with a train of British Railways Mark I stock on a Manchester–Marylebone working c1960, the same year in which express workings ceased to run over the Great Central London Extension. Note the immaculate condition of the station and the old fashioned 'Rothley' nameboard on the far left of the picture.

Rothley

The island platform as seen from under the road over-bridge with two of the station staff on the right of the 'down' line. The signal cabin in the background is now to be replaced by one from further down the Great Central, that at Blind Lane. At present the station is the terminus for the preserved steam railway and retains all its former charm.

Rothley

A four-coach local train from Nottingham to Leicester draws into Rothley station. The picture was taken from the road over-bridge which gave access to the platform. Note the deep cutting and the way the lines diverge to skirt the platform. the locomotive is of the K2 variety, though its number and depot are unidentifiable.

Rothley
1135 0-8-0 8a is seen here with a 'down' goods working at Rothley in 1922.

Belgrave & Birstall
Class 9P 4-6-0 No. 1167 *Lloyd George* (later nameless) passes Belgrave & Birstall with an 'up' Bradford train in 1921. The nameplates were said to have been removed for political reasons on the instructions of Sir Frederick Banbury, the then Chairman of the LNER. The train is made up of a 60-foot five-compartment brake Third, a 60-foot eight-compartment Third and a 60-foot restaurant car, which are the three vehicles visible in this picture.

Belgrave & Birstall
No. 185 Class 8 is seen here pulling away from Leicester towards Belgrave & Birstall and the Charnwood Forest country with a Leicester–Nottingham Victoria local in 1921. The only major place this train stopped at on its journey was Loughborough Central.

Belgrave & Birstall
A typical Great Central village with an unmetalled road down the centre and cobblestone pavements. This picture shows the main street which was just about all that went to make up the village. The building with the thatched roof in the foreground is the Old Plough Inn, noted for Sharpes Sileby ales.

Opposite
5506 Butler-Henderson stands at Leicester Central with an express for Marylebone.

Through the Heart of England

Under the canopy

Leicester Central station in its early days. This was an important hub in the Great Central network as demonstrated by the wide variety of destinations on the indicators. The departure times are shown by a series of clocks, forerunners of the modern electronic indicator boards. A ticket examiner sets one of the clocks. The decorative wrought iron is a typical feature of Victorian station architecture.

Chapter Four
THROUGH THE HEART OF ENGLAND LEICESTER TO WOODFORD

Leicester, dating back to Roman times when it was a small outpost on the Fosse Way, has always been an important centre of communications and has increased in size to become one of the largest industrial towns in England. Its trade was helped along by the Industrial Revolution, about which time the population almost trebled. However, since the thirteenth century Leicester had been recognised as a market town noted for its brewing and woollen industry. Knitwear and hosiery, which are two of the main trades today, were supplemented by the manufacture of footwear and the city is now the largest distributor for multiple companies producing these goods. Other industrial enterprises existed such

as brickmaking and the manufacture of elastic fabrics, yarns, cotton thread and typewriters, but the bias nowadays seems to have swung towards engineering. The towns prosperity had arisen mainly through the construction of a good transport network for conveying goods and raw materials. Later, with the advent of passenger trains, it was possible for traders to travel far and wide with their wares.

The first major improvement in transport in the Leicester area was the arrival of the Grand Union canal which was followed by the arrival of the Midland Railway which is still the main line today, although it, too, is a shadow of its former self. Leicester had three other stations which, sadly, are now all defunct and these were Belgrave Road, West Bridge and Central, showing the sheer volume of traffic created by the city.

'South Yorkshireman'
V2 4-6-2 60052 *Prince Palatine* leaves Leicester Central with a rake of Gresley and Thompson coaches on an 'up' 'South Yorkshireman' at 12.48pm. The train conveyed a refreshment car and only made stops at Rugby and Aylesbury on its way to London (Marylebone).

Lazy days at Leicester
GCR 4-4-2 No. 1085 stands in one of the bay platforms at Leicester Central just before the company was absorbed by the LNER. The illustration shows the footplate in clear detail.

Leicester Central was the London Extension station and was the last to be built in the city. Because it was midway between Manchester and Marylebone it was deemed to be an ideal location for a locomotive depot. The shed had four roads and could accommodate between fifteen and twenty engines depending on their size. 'Lester', as it was known in GC men's terms did not serve any major junction, its role was purely to provide relief engines for long haul goods and passenger workings, as well as providing engines for locals and shunting duties, in and around the goods yards and sidings at Abbey Lane. The shed was equipped with both a turntable and coaling stage, which remained unmechanised up until its sad demise in 1964. From the beginning, Leicester shed boasted a fine selection of engines for use on the London Extension.

These were the Robinson 'Atlantics', which gave stalwart performance on the lightly-loaded expresses of the new line. Their engine crews were formed mainly from men who had come from other parts of the MS&L network, but a fair proportion of men from local areas were taken on and trained, thus instilling the fine traditions of the Great Central upon Leicester folk. As the years went by, traffic began to be heavier but no significant changes were made to the stud until the time when the London North Eastern absorbed the Great Central at grouping. The standard of turnout of locomotives from Leicester was high from 1899 to 1964, which was not surprising considering the shed had a team of 70 men to maintain the engines on top of the coalers, labourers and youngsters employed. The early engines stationed on the Great

Leicester Central
Another B1 4-6-0 61224 makes light work of a York–Bournemouth train as it leaves Leicester Central on the long haul south. The variety of coaching stock and livery are noteworthy. The train standing in the bay platform is a B1 waiting on a local departure for Rugby. The mixture of semaphore and electric signalling is also worthy of mention.

Central at Leicester apart from the 'Atlantics' were the Class 9f+9h, Class 15 Sacres for local workings, and some Class 13s which remained for only a year after being transferred from Neasden. Indeed, some of the American 2-6-0s managed to arrive at Leicester and they were especially liked by drivers of the period due to their novel and luxurious design. For a short time the shed had an allocation of railcars which worked locals to Loughborough and Rugby and later, after some steaming prob-

lems, they were transferred to another part of the Great Central. Other locos which saw service at Leicester were the class 18s and a 9Q which worked the goods yard.

After grouping, the situation changed with the arrival of the 'Footballer' Class (LNER) which was to replace the 'Atlantics' which had been in service for over 30 years, but their power and ability did not match ther predecessors. However, it was not uncommon for them to achieve speeds in the 80s and 90s. A sequel to this design

Leicester Central
5509 *Prince Albert* is seen here coming off Leicester West bridge under an impressive array of signals into the throat of Leicester Central station, 29 June 1929. The stock is mixed, the first being a 60-foot compartment vehicle, while the others are of Gresley and early GC vintage.

was the building of the Thompson B1 4-6-0s which took place after the Second World War and they were the very last batch built by the LNER and were often seen on shed at Leicester or performing outstanding feats along various stretches of the line. In the ten years before the closure of Leicester Central shed, there was evidence of more powerful types like the V2s, A3s and B1s of which there were 38 and 8 respectively while goods and light duties were handled by 2 J11s and a J52. By 1963 the position was very different as the depot now played host to LMS types which had appeared as a result of the regional changes in 1958. The engine stud was now made up of 11 Class 5 'Staniers', 3 Class 4, 2-6-4 Staniers, 2 BR Class 5, 4-6-0s and an 0-6-0 diesel shunter. In 1964, after a slow and painful rundown through the many attempts to axe the shed, it finally closed leaving the men to seek employment 'Over the road'.

The station, on the other hand, was somewhat luckier as it survived until 1969, when the last vestige of a service disappeared. Like many of the other GC platforms, Leicester too was based on the island principle but as it was a larger station it incorporated two bays at the north and south ends of the station for local trains, while the outer platforms dealt with the main line traffic. The station was always a hive of activity as it was here that many trains made their engine change. One such train was the *South Yorkshireman* which took on a fresh engine and crew before continuing to its final destination. Because of its timing this train was one of the poorest revenue earners on the London Extension. The busiest time for the station was always on summer Saturdays when the line played host to the many holiday and cross-country workings, giving the enthusiast a fair range of locos to see, from GW 'Halls' and 'Granges' to the standard GC engines. On these days the lines around the station were usually stacked with as many as six relief engines for the latter type of workings. Moving out of Leicester Central it is possible to see a piece of the city's past before steaming through the area known as Aylestone Fields, and this is the Jewry Wall which dates back to the Roman times, a mass of stone-

Leicester
Deep in the heart of the city lay Carts Lane which was one of the early shopping areas, where it was possible to pick up boots, shoes and slippers made in the Midlands as well as fine hosiery and dress garments. The shop behind Richardson's appears to have something to do with funerals as the painting on the tower advertises wreathes and crosses. Judging by the parasol and the straw-boaters it is obviously a summer's day.

Abbey Lane
From the heavens it is possible to gain a fine view of the way the city is made up, with the decorative Abbey Park in the foreground behind which, and just out of the picture, lay the Great Central and some stabling sidings. At the top of the picture, amidst neatly arranged rows of terraced houses, one can make out the line of the Midland Railway, and it is also possible to see the station at Belgrave Road which was predominantly used by holiday excursion trains to Skegness and Mablethorpe.

Leicester loco
Leicester Central loco shed, beside which is a stores van. To the right, sheerlegs for lifting locos. A B1 4-6-0, 61298 waits on the middle road.

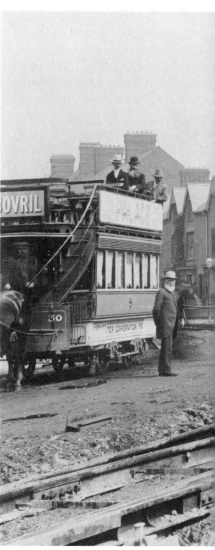

Leicester line-up
An impressive line-up at Leicester loco seen here on 12 March 1961. Leicester had a four-road engine shed and could accommodate 15 to 20 engines. It was used to supply engines for fast trains and some local workings, in addition to freight diagrams. In the background the massive power station, with its cooling-towers and generator building, dwarfs the locos which include two B1s and a Class 4MT.

The big upheaval
In preparation for the electric trams, massive engineering works are in progress to install the guide rails, while a horse tram passes on the left. Note the size of the rails and the curious retaining bars. Once the rails have been aligned, the road will be made up to its original level with metalling.

West Bridge

A fine view of Leicester showing the western entrance to the city. The city dated back to Roman times and was known as Ratae Coritanorum and here the Grand Union canal is seen from the point where it was crossed by the Great Central. Note the church and the ornate design of the road bridge over the canal.

Leicester

The market house and the corn exchange looking almost deserted. It was here where goods and wares made by Leicester's own factories would be exchanged. Note the statue which stands prominently in the middle of the square. The buildings have a somewhat continental look about them.

Market House and Corn Exchange

On shed – Leicester
76052, 4MT stands at Leicester loco, 22 August 1962, having just emerged from the shed.

Last days at Leicester
44835 arrives at Leicester Central with a train of BR Mk1 stock at platform 5. Already the two outer roads have been lifted where engines used to wait to relieve summer expresses in the line's busier days. The chalk markings on the locomotive were a special feature in the last years, with trains being given such exotic names as 'The Wild Thing', 'The Dick Flyer', 'The Woodford Belle' – a far cry from the official titles such as 'The Master Cutler' and 'The South Yorkshireman'.

Whetstone Bank
Robinson GCR Class 11B 4-4-0 No. 1035, built by Sharp Stewart in 1902 and later LNER Class D9, storms up the 1 in 176 of Whetstone Bank south of Leicester with the 10.30am special excursion from Nottingham Victoria to Marylebone on 26th March 1910.

work demonstrating the Roman lifestyle with its adjoining Forum and Roman Baths. Throughout the city the line was viaduct-borne and so the railway was one of the most prominent features amongst its industrial background. Sadly, very little remains today of the Great Central's viaducts and, indeed, the city has moved with the times, too, with its complexes of shopping centres and modern facilities, though the names De Montfort, Granby, and even Newton, to some extent will remain indelibly imprinted on the minds of many. Soon after Leicester the line breaks out towards Whetstone through open country.

Whetstone was the next stop along the route and, here again, the station followed the island-platform principle serving a small village which contained one large industrial area just off the Cosby Road. This complex was part of the General Electric Company who also had a works at Rugby which was served by sidings from the Great Central. It was at this Whetstone factory that work was done on the GT3 gas-turbine locomotive which underwent extensive trials on the London Extension. As usual, the station had its own goods facilities and the chief commodity dealt with here was domestic coal. Whetstone, due to its lack of ability (like Ashby Magna) to attract sufficient revenue, was one of the early casualities closing in 1963 with the withdrawal of local services. Just south of Whetstone, the line sweeps round a large bend which is known as Cosby Corner. From here onwards, as far as Ashby Magna, the railway passes through deep country on embankments and through cuttings whence it is only possible to see the odd house or village in the distance. Shortly after the line crosses the LNWR branch to Broughton Astley, to which a spur was built during the First World War to aid troop traffic and supplies. In 1959 another type of transport made its mark from Cosby Corner down to Shawell and this was Britain's first motorway, the M1. Ashby Magna station was not unlike that of Whetstone and it, too, served a small village with a meagre population, but there

Whetstone
Great Central double-header forming a Sunday excursion to Marylebone between Whetstone and Ashby Magna, with a fine head of steam coming from both locomotives. Here 'Atlantic' No. 192 is seen piloting 8C 4-6-0 No. 195. The stock is composed of three 'Barnum' saloons (which gain their name from being used on Barnum and Bailey Circus trains). The stock at the rear of the train is clerestory.

Whetstone
On a bright fine day an immaculately turned-out 11B 4-4-0 No. 1020 is seen here on an Oxford express having departed from Leicester at 10.58am. This area was known as Bluebanks spinney.

Cosby Corner

Typical of all villages in the area is Cosby, and in many ways similar to Whetstone which was actually served by the railway. This picture shows the old buildings that go to make up the main part of the village through the centre of which runs a stream, making the scene relatively timeless.

Ashby Magna

437 *Charles Stuart Wortley* on a Sheffield–Bournemouth working is seen here at Ashby Magna in 1920. No. 437 was one of the first series 'Directors' and was named after Charles Stuart Wortley who was a Director of the Railway from 1900 to 1922. He was created a Lord in 1917 and was also actually in office prior to 1900.

Ashby Magna

On 18 May 1963, 9F 2-10-0 is seen with a train of fish empties passing Ashby Magna signalbox and goods yard, where one can just make out the entrance to Dunton Bassett tunnel behind the sole mineral wagon standing in the sidings. The station had already been closed to passengers two months and though the 9Fs made a major contribution to the freight services on the line, they and their trains disappeared some two years later as part of the Beeching cuts.

Ashby Magna
One engine which fortunately has survived as a part of the National Collection is No. 506, later numbered 5506 in LNER days, *Butler Henderson* which performs regular on the short stretch of the old GC main line in Loughborough. Here *Butler Henderson* is seen at Ashby Magna in 192 in the prime of its life.

Peace and quiet
Ashby Magna station – a view looking towards Whetstone. The deserted single platform presages its impending doom.

Ashby Magna right away
A3 4-6-2 4472 *Flying Scotsman* is seen here steaming south with a GMRS Isle of Wigh Special on the 18 May 1963. This engine only appeared on the London Extension on special workings. Note the Metro Cammell pullman car which is leading the usual Mk1 stock. Under Great Central philosophy pullmans were thought to be unnecessary in the every day running as they believed their carriages were luxuriou enough and therefore did not require any embellishment in name or decor.

was no evidence of any industry in the area save for farming. Just south of the station the line entered a tunnel known as Dunton Bassett tunnel and this still stands today.

After a fairly straight run, which was one of the high-speed sections of the line, the route dipped down into the final port of call in Leicestershire at Lutterworth whose island platform was in view of the town's centrepiece, namely the church. Lutterworth is a small town with approximately 5,000 inhabitants and retains much of its original charm in the High Street.

One road still proclaims the name Station Road, though a journey along it soon reveals the stark truth. Only the stationmaster's house remains and the cutting where the yards and station stood. The signal box is worthy of note as it was a large structure for such a small station but it had been hoped to add extra lines, as apparent from the extra capacity which was available in the lever frame. The box closed at 03.50 on 13 June 1965, with the end of goods working on the London Extension. However, by far the most notable feature is

Last call before Rugby
44847, one of the ubiquitous class 5 MTs, leaves Lutterworth on an 'up' train on 15 July 1966. The building at the end of the platform was isolated from the others and an extra to the normal pattern of station buildings. The ornate lamp standard has been crudely updated with a modern light and a BR 'hotdog' symbol proclaiming Lutterworth.

A true island
Lutterworth station showing the layout of the buildings in their entirety. Nearest on the platform is the 'Gents', while the corrugated iron shed immediately behind was used for cycle storage. The adjacent building housed the waiting room and the 'Ladies'. The section with the canopy is the ticket office and the glass-covered area protects the stairway up from the road to the platform. The house in the background belonged to the stationmaster. The A40 car in the yard helps to date the scene.

'Halls' and fish trains
4937 'Hall' Class, resplendent in all respects, works an 'up' Swindon 'fish' and is seen charging along towards the viaduct over the LNWR at Rugby. The stock comprises ventilated vans and one container vehicle (ninth one along).

Lutterworth
A5 69818 works an 'up' local near Lutterworth with a four-coach train. The cloud of steam provides an ethereal atmosphere.

the church of which John Wycliffe was rector for twenty years until his death in 1384. Thirty years later his doctrines were dispensed with by the Council of Constance, and his remains were disinterred, burnt and scattered in the town's river, the Swift. He is now remembered for having promoted the translation of the Bible into the common tongue. Such is Lutterworth's claim to fame.

Dropping down towards Shawell, the line soon brings the approaches of Rugby into view and the Avon viaduct which crossed the river Avon and its plain before arriving at the 'Birdcage' bridge – which crossed the massive fourteen tracks of the main Rugby station complex which belonged to the route to the north from Euston. The 'Birdcage' bridge caused a problem for the Great Central

soon after its construction as it obscured the view of one of the signal gantries from the signal box at Clifton Mill Junction. As a result, the Great Central had to provide an extra row of aspects for the gantry in question and when completed, it gained the nickname 'Bedstead', due to the amount of metalwork. Shortly after the 'Birdcage' bridge the line ran along a short embankment and then entered a deep cutting surrounded by the Hillmorton district of Rugby. After passing under a roadbridge the station appeared, a rather less grand affair than its counterpart. Rugby Central was the halfway point of the London Extension and was also one of the stops for express trains and the changeover point for local services. At the time of closure in 1966, Rugby became the most southerly station on the commuter service to Nottingham, which was the last vestige of life on the Great Central. Rugby, with its population of roughly 57,000, had ample justification for two stations, and indeed with the town's railway and engineering works the Great Central provided a much valued connection to the GEC factory. In its heyday the station's own yard provided a vital link to other places and a transfer point for the many goods brought into the town. Another set of sidings existed at Barby, just to the south of Rugby, and these had been installed during the Second World War by the LNER to serve a war department depot and it was at this spot that an accident occurred on 7 August 1955. On this occasion, the between-Rugby-and-Barby was subject to single line working regulations and it was realised that a crossover at Barby could be used, thus reducing the single line section; this cross-over had, in fact, been scheduled to be removed and was subject to a 15 mph speed restriction and consequently when the 10.35 train from Manchester to Maryle-bone took it at 55 mph the whole train derailed and plunged down the embankment killing the driver and injuring several passengers.

Returning to Rugby itself, the town dates back to the times of the Saxons and it was originally just a small hamlet of the Clifton-upon-Dunsmore parish through which the Great Central traversed. Rugby did not become important until

48157 is seen here approaching Rugby Central with an engineers' train.

Rugby requiem
On a fine day in July 1966, 44920 steams into Rugby with a 'down' Nottingham train to pick up a handful of passengers. A special feature of Rugby Central, like Brackley, was the elaborate entrance hall and stairway to the platforms.

Rugby 'Runner'
9F 92132 having just crossed the massive viaduct over the Avon and the 'Birdcage' bridge, steams along the last lap to Rugby Central station with a Woodford freight.

Victorian times, mainly because of the advent of the railways and one of the things which benefited the Central station was the close proximity of Rugby School which was established in 1567 by Laurence Sheriff. The original school, however, was moved to the south side of the town to its present location and was rebuilt in 1809. Rugby School, apart from being a top public school, was probably best known for its invention of the game named after it, and its Headmaster, Dr Arnold (a school reformer) who was described by Thomas Hughes, one of his pupils, in *Tom Brown's Schooldays*. On leaving Rugby and returning to open country, the railway came in sight of the GPO Radio Station with its 820-foot masts. Because of their height and red warning lights, these masts were a marker for trains stopping at the station at night during the latter years of the line.

Having crossed the Warwickshire border the line entered the

Stopping train
Rugby Central, from the Staverton end, showing J11, 64327 pulling some unusual stock on an evening local in September 1954. The first vehicle is an ex Great Northern six-wheeled full brake van, while the second is of GC vintage. The rest of the train is made up of Gressley stock.

Rugby South
An impressive display as V2 60108, *Gay Crusader*, storms away from Rugby Central in clouds of smoke with the 'up' 'Master Cutler'. It hauls a splendid rake of BR Mk1 coaches in 'blood and custard' livery. The engine was a stranger to the GC and is only known to have worked on the line on a few occasions, as did sister engine 60103, 'The Flying Scotsman'.

Braunston & Willoughby
No. 6094, a C4 'Atlantic', is seen on a passenger express in 1928.

Braunston & Willoughby
No. 5504 *Jutland* passes Braunston &
Willoughby station on a parcels working in
1928. The station was originally named
Willoughby before being lengthened to
Braunston & Willoughby in 1904.

Braunston & Willoughby
No. 6257, an 04 Class, works a local goods
in the same year. When the station was
first built Colonel John Henry Lowndes
thought that a direct line to Leicester from
his own village would boost the local shoe
industry, and would make the carriage of
milk and livestock to London and Leicester
a worthwhile proposition.

Staverton Road
Goods traffic was always fairly heavy on
the London Extension and here one of the
freight workhorses 013476 works an 'up'
freight towards Staverton signal cabin.

100

Northamptonshire countryside before re-entering Warwickshire to call at the wayside station of Braunston & Willoughby, which lay on the Daventry Road. From the county boundary to the station itself the line followed the course of the Oxford Canal, which was bridged at Rugby by the London Extension. Braunston & Willoughby was one of the early casualties for closure along with Culworth in the late 1950s. The station did not attract enough revenue for its local service and

this was known as early as July 1904, when the station changed its name from just plain Willoughby to Braunston & Willoughby in the hope of attracting a better patronage from slightly further afield. From Braunston the line began a steady climb through the Northamptonshire uplands as far as Charwelton. Just past the little village of Flecknoe was Staverton Road signal box which was fairly isolated, approximately halfway along the climb, and this box was oil-lit right up until closure. After

Locos on trial
But for the signal box which displays the name Staverton Road, it is hard to imagine that this shot was taken on the GC. The engine is SR 'Bulleid West Country Pacific' 34006 *Bude* with a 'down' express on 16 June 1948. The headcode, unlike those of the GC, is made up of two white discs, and the tender on the engine belongs to a Black Five.

Staverton Road
V2 4474 *Victor Wild* climbs Staverton Bank with an 'up' express made up of Gressley teak stock.

'Windcutter'
One rather misty day in March 1962, 9F 92094 with a heavy train of loaded coal wagons and vans, approaches Charwelton yard. In the background one can just make out the entrance to Catesby tunnel and one of its breathers.

crossing Staverton Road and a series of viaducts, the line approached a deep cutting which led to the Northern Portal of Catesby tunnel and it was this stretch down the Leam valley from Braunston & Willoughby that the 'Runners' and 'Windcutters' used to achieve speeds of 50 or 60 mph as it was almost a straight run down to Woodford.

Catesby tunnel lies underneath the home of Robert Catesby who was known for his part in the Gunpowder Plot, and he was supposed to have been the chief instigator in trying to blow up the Houses of Parliament. Fortunately the plot was foiled and he and his fellow conspirators were rounded up and executed. By the time the railway arrived, a long tunnel had had to be built so that the line could not be seen by the occupants of the estate and this was how the 3,000 yard tunnel of shallow bore came into use. Inside, the tunnel contained millions of bricks and it dripped soot-stained water which made conditions extremely wet and, though devoid of life, it has not changed much today.

Catesby
V2 60863, with a Newcastle–Bournemouth train of SR stock, emerges from Catesby tunnel on a fine September day in 1961. Above is seen one of the ventilation shafts of the 3,000-yard-long tunnel.

Legend has it that the tunnel may even have been haunted. There were some unexplained happenings, like the incident which occurred a few days prior to Christmas 1963. A driver of an 'Up' express reported to his control station that his engine had been struck by an object which had bent the handrail, but on inspection near the tunnel mouth nothing was found by the men from Charwelton. A later train crew also confirmed that nothing was amiss.

Emerging from the southern portal, the line wended its way out of a cutting and under a roadbridge into the busy little station of Charwelton, which was the exchange point for ironstone trains from the local quarry. Indeed, it was not unusual for a total of 220 wagons to be stabled in the yard. In a typical day in the working of Charwelton, no fewer than eighteen trains passed the cabin in addition to the passenger trains. Goods trains using the yard would arrive with up to fifty wagons a piece. Even up to the decline of the railway in 1963, when Charwelton station closed, the yard was still busy with goods traffic. However, the passing of the station was mourned by few,

Top
Charwelton
On a spring day in 1962, L1 67789, draws away from Charwelton with a two-coach local train for Rugby. Note the large number of mineral wagons in the sidings which served the nearby ironstone workings. An old-fashioned AEC Daimler bus crosses the bridge.

Bottom
Deep in the Northamptonshire uplands
B1 61083, resplendent in BR lines black livery, passes Charwelton signalbox and yard with a 'down' Manchester express. The station lies in the background and the rural catchment area says it all.

save those employed at the ironstone workings. As one local farmer told me, the most chaotic week for the railway was the Charwelton Week which took place every June. One such week in 1958 was particularly memorable as the line suffered from an abundance of livestock rather than rolling stock, as cattle were reported on the line on several occasions and some even paid homage to the water troughs which lay to the south of the station. These troughs, not intended for cattle, were placed on the sleepers in between the rails where the locomotives could pick up water at high speeds. The troughs were supplied from a large tank at the side of the railway and water was pumped up from the river Cherwell which rose in the cellars of an old farmhouse. In order to prevent the water from freezing in cold

spells, the Great Central had installed a steampipe which ran the length of each trough. The fireman picked up water from them by turning a handle at the top of a vertical pipe at the corner of the tender. The pipe was perforated with a series of holes and operated a scoop which took up the water. After taking on water, the fireman turned the large handle again until it returned to its original position and then replaced the chain and spouting pipe whereupon the flow stopped and the tension on the apparatus was released.

Along the line, the horizon opens out and a massive complex of buildings and railway lines are visible. This is Woodford and Hinton (later changed to Woodford Halse at the request of the Parish Council in 1947) where the inhabitants live and breathe railways.

Watering time
No. 5505 *Ypres* often pronounced 'Wipers', in a cloud of spray, takes on water from the Charwelton troughs, on its way to Sheffield.

Opposite
WD Class 'Austerity' 2-8-0, 90433 is seen at Woodford Halse with an up mixed goods.

Woodford to Quainton

Woodford loco
In the early days of the line, a loco crew poses for a group photograph in front of a resplendent engine, No. 867: the well dressed man by the number is Mr Sherriff, the loco inspector. Note the large and the semi-open footplate. These engines, with their smartly turned out coaches, were the mainstay of the London Extension and made light work of hauling expresses.

Chapter Five

WOODFORD TO QUAINTON

Woodford Halse, the nerve centre of operations for the Great Central's London Extension, was one of the five depots on the London-Sheffield route, the others being Colwick, Neasden, Annesley and Leicester. It was better known as a 'Railway Village' in the country. Situated amidst trees, hills, streams and tranquil countryside, Woodford lay twelve miles from Northampton and eight miles from Banbury which were the two nearest large centres before the arrival of the railway. At the time of the authorisation of the railway, Woodford was a typical small dwelling area of some sixty-one houses and one of three villages which made up the parish of Woodford-cum-Membris. There was an ideal site, not only for the actual railway but

for a depot, a site for marshalling vehicles, servicing, storage and fuel supplies. The idea was to bring great benefit to Woodford by providing an opportunity to gain access to the East & West Junction Railway, providing a link to Stratford-upon-Avon and Northampton, and this was achieved admirably. Later a connection was to be made to Banbury and in this way a whole range of destinations were available as the line's importance grew for both passengers and freight. From the outset Woodford Halse was designated as a site for a station because of the decision to build a depot and a railway community around it, but this left Byfield and Moreton Pinkney on the East & West Junction Railway as secondary stations on what was considered a rather tortuous route. Later this reputation earned it the nickname 'Slow & Muddle Junction' when it came under the control of the Stratford & Midland Junction Railway.

So, to say that Woodford encountered little change would be an understatement. In this predominantly agricultural area, as the census shows for 1891 (see Appendix), cottage industries still accounted for a great number of the workforce, while 4,329 people are recorded as working on the railways for the same period in Northamptonshire. The major factor for the drift away was improved pay and better conditions. By 1901 the number of railway employees had increased by just over a thousand probably due to the arrival of the Great Central London Extension at Woodford.

Naturally the inhabitants of Woodford objected most strongly to the railway and the depot, and when it was proposed to build rows of terraced houses for the workers it was said that they would ruin the village's atmosphere. Thus Woodford became, in effect, two communities: 'railway' and 'country'. Although this is no

longer the case, the original division is reflected in the two different types of houses in the village. Within the railway community there was a social ladder akin to the class system, which depended upon the nature of employment. The stationmaster, regarded on a par with the doctor, squire and clergyman, was at the top of the scale, while other workers' status was also defined by the type of accommodation – especially the size of house which varied according to the employment. Engine drivers' houses were spacious, well situated with a view, and all their homes had bay windows with suitable space for a piano, and so the road became known as 'Piano Row' by the locals. Porters and other employees further down the scale were proportionately less well accommodated. The latter mainly lived in the roads below the embankment such as Percy and Sidney Roads. Another sort of housing appeared in 1907 and

Woodford & Hinton
The station was later renamed Woodford Halse on 1 November 1948, but here the date is 1925 and D11 5508 *The Prince of Wales* is on an 'up' express to Marylebone from Manchester. 5508 was one of eleven engines built between 1919 and 1930 known as the 'Director' Class and they were an update on the D10 design. These engines were employed on the toughest schedules on the London Extension and continued to provide stalwart service right into the 1950s.

Woodford – The shed *Opposite top*
An impressive line-up on 13 December 1936 with ex Great Northern 'Atlantic' No. 3293, seen here steaming up. The latter engines enjoyed a short spell on the Central in the 1930s working long distance trains. The engine behind is LNER (ex. GC) C4 'Atlantic' 6078, while two unidentified types stand by the water column in the background.

Woodford – The shed *Opposite bottom*
Inside the shed two Great Central workhorses await their turn of duty while another, on the left, fully coaled up, prepares for off. Note the continuous hoods for smoke extraction and the gas lamp above 867's tender. The shed was designed to admit the maximum amount of light and air. The importance of Woodford can be deduced from the lack of motive power in the shed when the photograph was taken.

this was caused by the increase in longhaul traffic. A set of lodgings was provided for guards, firemen and drivers from foreign depots. The lodgings were four houses amidst the 136 terraced houses in which Woodford's workers lived and they continued to be occupied until the Second World War, when they became solely for the use of locomotive crews based at Woodford.

Turning to the station itself, this was built on the 'island' formation and access was gained from a staircase leading up to the platform from Station Road. This staircase unfortunately is now sealed into the overbridge which carried the main lines either side, and the platform and buildings have now been levelled, too. In its prime the platform at Woodford boasted four blocks of buildings which contained the usual facilities: toilets, cycle and store sheds, waiting rooms and a porter's room. At the northern end was a small cabin at the rear of the staff exit. The station also had a refreshment room but this was closed in 1954 owing to a falling off in patronage. When the Banbury link was introduced, the extra wooden platform provided a setdown and pick-up point without interfering with the main line. The line through this platform served Byfield and originally it was part of the loop into the yards. In 1956, around the time of the British Rail moderni-

sation plan, the platform was replaced by a concrete structure.

North of the station lay the marshalling yards which extended over a site of thirty-five acres and they were constructed from spoil taken from the excavation of Catesby tunnel. In the east yard the depot was built with an engine shed that had capacity for thirty locomotives, a snowplough and a crane. From the beginning, Woodford was the stabling point for some of the finest locomotives turned out by the Great Central and later the London North Eastern Railway. Harry Pollitt, the first locomotive engineer for the new Great Central empire, had been building engines suitable for the longer runs since 1894 but it was not until 1900 that a significant step was made to make the line efficient, when J. G. Robinson was appointed. Several of his splendid designs were at Woodford Halse in the early years, such as the J9 0-6-0 and 04 2-8-0 'Tinies' for goods and the 11B 4-4-0 for express passenger work. A more powerful design was the 11E or 'Director' Class whose excellence and performance kept them going even into the Gresley and Thompson era. Indeed, more were added to their number for this reason alone. In the years of the two LNER designers, the 'Atlantics' and B7s regularly employed on fish trains, gave way to B1 4-6-0s and B5s which became regular performers on BR in later

Woodford & Hinton
On a grey day in 1925, No. 5219 of the J11 Class works an 'up' goods at Woodford. The J11s were affectionately known as 'Pom Poms' and were used primarily on goods trains although, like most of the other 0-6-0 Classes, they saw occasional use on passenger workings. 174 of the Class were built, with the first engine No. 973 appearing in 1901.

years. By 1950 Woodford had a fair selection of LNER locos, some of which had been built by the Great Central, like the J39, J11, N2 and N5 of which there were ten, two, one and five respectively. Moving into the more powerful league, there were four B17 4-6-0s and 10 V2 2-6-2s. Of course the depot also hosted some 'odd-birds' like the ex War Department engines which totalled 54 in number.

However, the whole situation changed in 1958 at Woodford with the incorporation of the London Extension in to the Midland Region of British Railways which brought with it an influx of ex LMS types and this is borne out by the table below, which shows the loco-motives stabled at Woodford over the last ten years.

Type	1955	1959	1963	1965*
B1 4-6-0	3	5	2	44835
J11 0-6-0	8	—	—	48002
L1 2-6-4T	1	3	—	48010
L3 2-6-4T	1	—	—	48035
V2 2-6-2	6	3	—	48121
WD 2-8-0	25	26	23	42082
K3 2-6-0	8	—	—	*last six
Class 4 2-6-0	—	2	—	on shed at
Class 3F 0-6-0	—	3	—	closure
Shunter Diesel 0-6-0	—	4	4	
Class 8F 2-8-0	—	—	3	
Class 5 4-6-0-	—	—	5	
Class 4 2-6-4	—	—	7	
(BR)C14 4-6-0	—	—	3	
(BR)C15 4-6-0	—	—	7	

Apart from the engines listed above, another regular visitor was the 9F Class which was employed on the intensive freight trips between Annesely and Woodford. These engines were nick-named 'Runners' and 'Windcutters' due to their swiftness. Woodford was most noted for its freight trains and in the early years Great Central drivers carried fish and steel, mainly on lodging turns, as well as coal. It was not unknown for train crews to receive 'perks' from these loads. The fish came from Grimsby while the steel traffic was important to Sheffield's chief industry – the manufacture of cutlery and domestic utensils. Coal was needed for internal and external use as it not only provided fuel for the loco-motives but also a much sought after form of energy for industry. Coal traffic thus ensured

a staple revenue for the Great Central. Woodford also provided a wagon exchange point for other major companies in the area, such as the Great Western and the East & West Junction Railway, whose complex connecting lines south of the station made it possible for the Great Central to handle long-distance trains to Wales and Tyneside and many other such destinations. Whilst in the 40s there were 16 full trains of freight from Woodford to Banbury every 24 hours, there was never more than a few wagons daily to the East & West Junction Railway (later Stratford and Midland Junction) as it was mainly used as a through route. The Junction was laid out as opposite, although the Stratford connection was taken out in 1900 soon after the railway was built.

By far the most important part of Woodford's claim to fame was the marshalling yards which took the appearance of the illustration opposite, although the new marshalling yards were not added until after the beginning of the Second World War to cope with some of the extra traffic. The two new yards had 16 'down' and 12 'up' sidings. Indeed, this addition was very useful in 1947 when BR introduced their fast freight service running between Annesley and Woodford, comprising 40 trains which ran with precision timing before returning with other trains; they were an unbeatable service and well deserved their titles adopted at the time the 9Fs were draughted in. One strange feature, by the loco depot, was a triangle for turning engines rather than a turntable and seemed rather an elaborate operation. In the vicinity of the triangle was the coaling plant and on the other side of the loco were the carriage and wagon shops which were responsible for carrying out repairs. To aid this process, a traverser was provided at the north end so the wagons could be run in to the shop according to the repair needed.

Woodford Halse was a large community and it has a history which nowadays is relived regularly at the Woodford Halse Social Club, a black and white timber

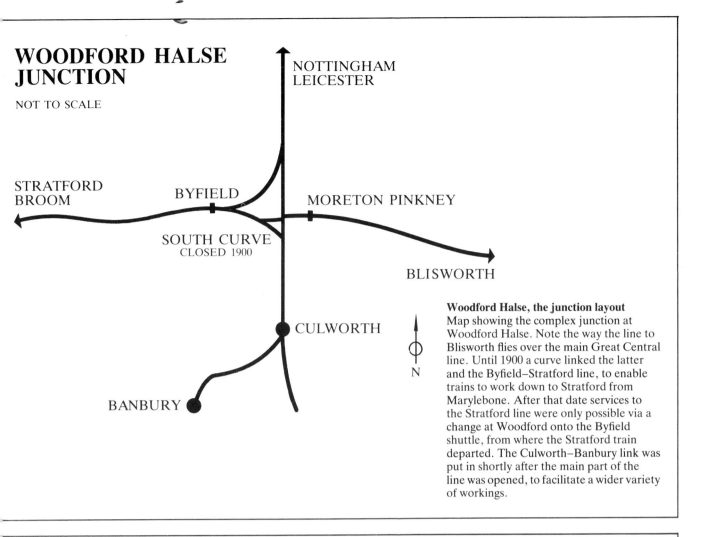

WOODFORD HALSE JUNCTION

NOT TO SCALE

NOTTINGHAM
LEICESTER

STRATFORD
BROOM

BYFIELD

MORETON PINKNEY

SOUTH CURVE
CLOSED 1900

BLISWORTH

CULWORTH

BANBURY

N

Woodford Halse, the junction layout
Map showing the complex junction at Woodford Halse. Note the way the line to Blisworth flies over the main Great Central line. Until 1900 a curve linked the latter and the Byfield–Stratford line, to enable trains to work down to Stratford from Marylebone. After that date services to the Stratford line were only possible via a change at Woodford onto the Byfield shuttle, from where the Stratford train departed. The Culworth–Banbury link was put in shortly after the main part of the line was opened, to facilitate a wider variety of workings.

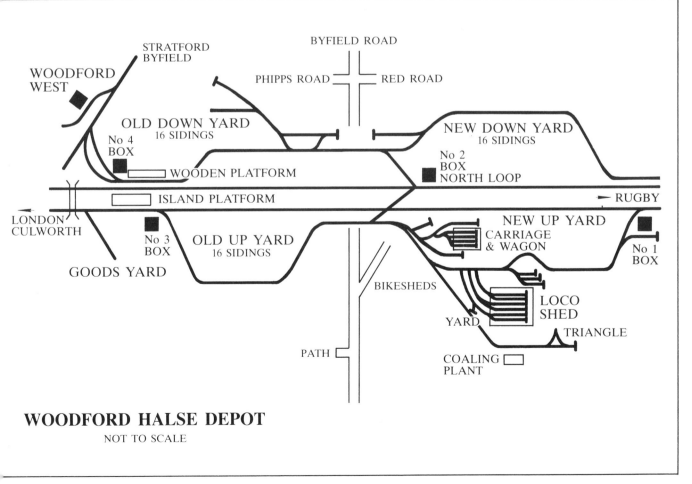

STRATFORD
BYFIELD

BYFIELD ROAD

WOODFORD
WEST

PHIPPS ROAD

RED ROAD

OLD DOWN YARD
16 SIDINGS

No 4
BOX

WOODEN PLATFORM

NEW DOWN YARD
16 SIDINGS

No 2
BOX
NORTH LOOP

ISLAND PLATFORM

RUGBY

LONDON
CULWORTH

No 3
BOX

OLD UP YARD
16 SIDINGS

NEW UP YARD

CARRIAGE
& WAGON

No 1
BOX

GOODS YARD

BIKESHEDS

YARD

LOCO
SHED

TRIANGLE

PATH

COALING
PLANT

WOODFORD HALSE DEPOT

NOT TO SCALE

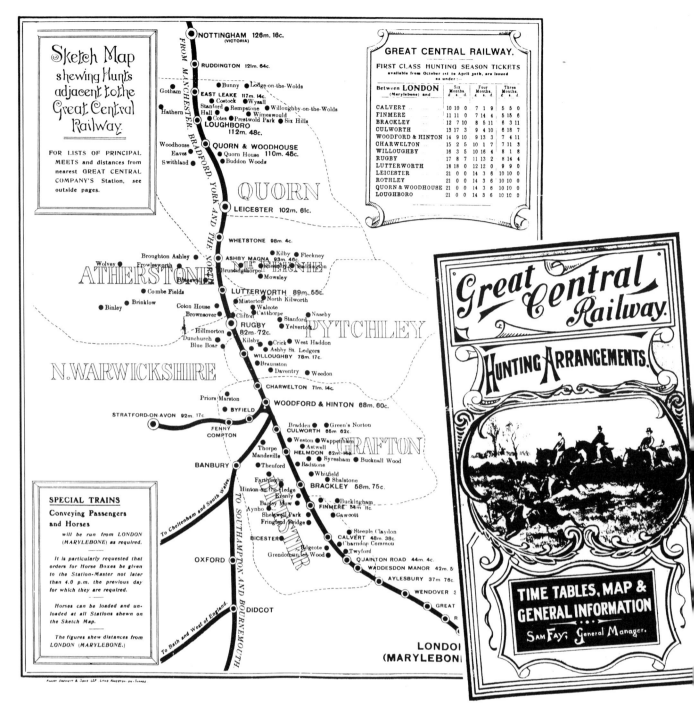

building which is a prominent feature of the village. The Club has a story all of its own, mostly connected with the railway. In its early days it was known as the Hinton Gorse and was well frequented by the hunting fraternity who also took advantage of the station facilities. On hunt days, the Great Central laid on special services to convey the horses, dogs, and attendants to cater for every whim of their riders. But by the early 1950s the building had been acquired for railway purposes and in 1953 the Hinton Gorse came under the auspices of the British Rail Staff Association and many social events took place there for local railway employees. Sadly, this situation only lasted for ten years as the railway club's role became redundant after the closure of the depot, the implications of which are explained in the next chapter. Since 1976 the enthusiasm of former employees has ensured that some part of Woodford's history is retained and what better place to go for entertainment or a film evening than a club where one can turn the clock back thirty years and listen to the nostalgic reminiscences of retired enginemen.

Easing out of Woodford and its complex junction, the line trundled over an embankment through more lush Northamptonshire country-

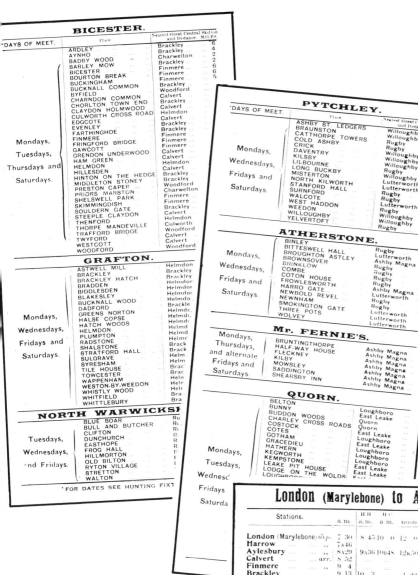

BICESTER.

DAYS OF MEET.	Place	Nearest Great Central Station and Distance. MILES
Mondays, Tuesdays, Thursdays and Saturdays.	ARDLEY	Brackley ... 6
	AYNHO	Brackley ... 4
	BADBY WOOD	Charwelton ... 2
	BARLEY MOW	Brackley ... 2
	BICESTER	Finmere ... 6
	BOURTON BREAK	Finmere ... 6
	BUCKINGHAM	Finmere ... 5
	BUCKNALL COMMON	Brackley ...
	BYFIELD	Calvert ...
	CHARNDON COMMON	Brackley ...
	CHORLTON TOWN END	Calvert ...
	CLAYDON HOLMWOOD	Helmdon ...
	CULWORTH CROSS ROAD	Helmdon ...
	EDGCOTE	Brackley ...
	EVENLEY	Brackley ...
	FARTHINGHOE	Finmere ...
	FINMERE	Finmere ...
	FRINGFORD BRIDGE	Finmere ...
	GAWCOTT	Calvert ...
	GRENDON UNDERWOOD	Calvert ...
	HAM GREEN	Helmdon ...
	HELMDON	Calvert ...
	HILLESDEN	Brackley ...
	HINTON ON THE HEDGE	Brackley ...
	MIDDLETON STONEY	Woodford ...
	PRESTON CAPER	Charwelton ...
	PRIORS MARSTON	Finmere ...
	SHELSWELL PARK	Finmere ...
	SKIMMINGDISH	Brackley ...
	SOULDERN GATE	Calvert ...
	STEEPLE CLAYDON	Helmdon ...
	THENFORD	Culworth ...
	THORPE MANDEVILLE	Woodford ...
	TRAFFORD BRIDGE	Calvert ...
	TWYFORD	Calvert ...
	WESTCOTT	Woodford ...
	WOODFORD	

GRAFTON.

	Place	
Mondays, Wednesdays, Fridays and Saturdays.	ASTWELL MILL	Helmdon
	BRACKLEY	Brackley
	BRACKLEY HATCH	Helmdon
	BRADDEN	Helmdon
	BIDDLESDEN	Helmdon
	BLAKESLEY	Helmdo
	BUCKNALL WOOD	Brackle
	DADFORD	Helmdo
	GREENS NORTON	Helmdo
	HALSE COPSE	Helmdo
	HATCH WOODS	Helmd
	HELMDON	Helmd
	PLUMPTON	Helmc
	RADSTONE	Brack
	SHALSTONE	Brack
	STRATFORD HALL	Helm
	SULGRAVE	Helm
	SYRESHAM	Helm
	TILE HOUSE	Brac
	TOWCESTER	Brac
	WAPPENHAM	Helr
	WESTON-BY-WEEDON	Helr
	WHISTLY WOOD	Bra
	WHITFIELD	Bra
	WHITTLEBURY	Bra

NORTH WARWICKSH

	Place	
Tuesdays, Wednesdays, ~~and~~ Fridays.	BLUE BOAR	Ru
	BULL AND BUTCHER	Ru
	CLIFTON	R.
	DUNCHURCH	R.
	EASTHOPE	R
	FROG HALL	F
	HILLMORTON	F
	OLD BILTON	
	RYTON VILLAGE	
	STRETTON	
	WALTON	

FOR DATES SEE HUNTING FIXT

PYTCHLEY.

DAYS OF MEET.	Place	Nearest Great Central and Distance. M
Mondays, Wednesdays, Fridays and Saturdays.	ASHBY ST. LEDGERS	Willoughby
	BRAUNSTON	Willoughby
	CATTHORPE TOWERS	Rugby
	COLD ASHBY	Rugby
	CRICK	Rugby
	DAVENTRY	Willoughby
	KILSBY	Willoughby
	LILBOURNE	Willoughby
	LONG BUCKBY	Rugby
	MISTERTON	Willoughby
	NORTH KILWORTH	Lutterworth
	STANFORD HALL	Lutterworth
	SURNFORD	Rugby
	WALCOTE	Rugby
	WEST HADDON	Lutterworth
	WEEDON	Rugby
	WILLOUGHBY	Willoughby
	YELVERTOFT	Rugby

ATHERSTONE.

Mondays, Wednesdays, Fridays and Saturdays.	BINLEY	Rugby
	BITTESWELL HALL	Lutterworth
	BROUGHTON ASTLEY	Ashby Magna
	BROWNSOVER	Rugby
	BRINKLOW	Rugby
	COMBE	Rugby
	COTON HOUSE	Rugby
	FROWLESWORTH	Ashby Magna
	HARRO GATE	Lutterworth
	NEWBOLD REVEL	Rugby
	NEWNHAM	Rugby
	SMOKINGTON GATE	Lutterworth
	THREE POTS	Lutterworth
	WOLVEY	Lutterworth

Mr. FERNIE'S.

	Place	
Mondays, Thursdays, and alternate Fridays and Saturdays.	BRUNTINGTHORPE	Ashby Magna
	HALF-WAY HOUSE	Ashby Magna
	FLECKNEY	Ashby Magna
	KILBY	Ashby Magna
	MOWSLEY	Ashby Magna
	SADDINGTON	Ashby Magna
	SHEARSBY INN	Ashby Magna

QUORN.

Mondays, Tuesdays, Wednesd Fridays Saturda	BELTON	Loughboro
	BUNNY	East Leake
	BUDDON WOODS	Quorn
	CHARLEY CROSS ROADS	Quorn
	COSTOCK	East Leake
	COTES	Loughboro
	GOTHAM	East Leake
	GRACEDIEU	Loughboro
	HATHERN	Loughboro
	KEGWORTH	Loughboro
	KEMPSTONE	Loughboro
	LEAKE PIT HOUSE	East Leake
	LODGE ON THE WOLDS	East Leake
	LOUGHBORO	East

Tally ho!

One of the ways in which the Great Central went about attracting people to travel on its new line was through its vast publicity department, and this illustration shows an example of one of the ways of taking advantage of the line's scenic beauty. This leaflet shows hunts adjacent to the Great Central and the company laid on special facilities, tickets and trains for both the horses and their riders. One of the areas noted for its hunt was Finmere in the Bicester hunt country. Indeed, the Great Central even made provision for the local hunt at the time the station was being built, when they constructed a wooden overbridge in a cutting just to the north of the station.

side, before approaching a lone standing signal box near the village of Culworth where the link to Banbury branched off. Unfortunately, because of the course of the line, Culworth station was in fact nearer Moreton Pinkney which was already served by another company. However, for the villagers the halt at Eydon Road on the Banbury line was more convenient. It was this line that played a strategic role in the movement of munitions, war materials and troops. With the cessation of hostilities the Great Central, like other companies, had to pick up the pieces from a noticeably decreased stock and rundown system. By the

London (Marylebone) to Aylesbury, Brackley, Rugby, Leicester, etc.

Stations.	a.m.	H H a.m.	H C a.m.	noon	p.m.	p.m.	p.m.	p.m.	H C p.m.	H C p.m.	p.m.	p.m.	p.m.	
London (Marylebone) *dep.*	7 30	8 45	10 0	12 0	12 8	1 40	4 0	4 30	5 40	6 5	7 30	10 0		A—Stops to set down passengers from London or take up for G.C. line.
Harrow	7 46			12 24		4 15				6 21	7 46	10 16		B—Stops when required to take up passengers for Leicester or beyond on notice being given at Aylesbury.
Aylesbury	8 29	9 36	10 48	12 50	1 8 7	2 30	4 54			7 8	8 29	10 58		C—Through carriages London (Marylebone) to Stratford-on-Avon.
Calvert	8 52				1 25					7 31	T			D—Stops when required to set down passengers from London or beyond on notice being given to the guard at Woodford.
Finmere	9 4				1 37		5 16			7 44	8 51			E—Stops when required to set down passengers from London or Aylesbury on notice being given to the guard at Brackley.
Brackley	9 13	10 3		1 22	1 46		5 23		7 0	7 54	9 1			H—Stops when required to take up passengers from the G.W. or Metropolitan lines on notice being given at Aylesbury.
Helmdon	9 21				1 54		6 8			8 3				HC—Horse-boxes and carriage traffic conveyed by these trains.
Culworth	9 31				2 2		6 16			8 12				H H—Horse-box traffic not to be conveyed between intermediate stations by this train.
Woodford	9 37	E 11 29	1 34	2 8		6 22			7 9	8 19				K—Stops when required to take up passengers for Brackley or beyond on notice being given at Aylesbury.
Byfield									7 16					P—Stops when required to take up passengers for Finmere or beyond on notice being given at the station.
Fenny Compton				T					T					T—Stops when required to set down passengers on notice being given at the preceding stopping-station.
Stratford-on-Avon			12 28	2 25					S C 0					W—Stops on Saturdays only when required to set down passengers from London on notice being given to the guard at Marylebone.
Charlwelton	9 43						6 28			8 25				
Willoughby	9 54					2 26	5 49			8 37				
Rugby	10 2	10 33	11 w42	1 54	2 35		5 57		P	8 46	9 34	11 57		
Lutterworth	10 27	10 50			2 45		6 7			8 56	9 44			
Ashby Magna	10 58				2 53					9 4	10 40			
Whetstone	11 7						7 16			9 13	10 49			
Leicester	10 44	10 55	12	2 17	3 10	3 40	6 22	6 33	7 49	9 21	10 1	12 21		
Quorn & Woodhouse	11 46	12 32	3 11		4 11		7 6	8 31		10 21				
Loughboro'	11 2	11 51	12 37	2 36		4 16	6 38	7 11	8 36		10 26			
East Leake		12 0	12 46	3 25		4 25		7 20	8 45		10 35			
Nottingham	11 22	11 27	12 40	2 53		4 11	6 57	7 5	8 21		10 56	12 55		

★ Slip Coach from November 1st.

UP TRAINS

Leicester, Rugby, Brackley, Aylesbury, etc., to London (Marylebone).

Stations.	a.m.	a.m.	a.m.	a.m.	H H a.m.	H C a.m.	p.m.	p.m.	p.m.	p.m.	p.m.	H C p.m.	a.m.	
Nottingham *dep.*	5 50	7 45		8 52	10 21	12 12	12 21	2 32	4 8	5 25	7 12	12 27		A—Stops when required to take up passengers.
East Leake		7 10		8 10	6	11 57	12 41	2 15	3 56	4 40	6 31	11 26		B—Stops when required to set down passengers from G.C. line, or take up for London.
Loughboro'	6 10	8 4		9 12	10 45	9	12 50	2 23	5 4		6 40	11 35		C—Through carriage Stratford-on-Avon to London (Marylebone).
Quorn & Woodhouse		7 24		8 22	10 20		12 11	12 55	2 29	4 10	4 54	6 45	11 40	D—Stops when required to take up passengers for London (Marylebone) on notice being given at the station.
Leicester	6 40	8 20	8 25	9 30	10 52	12 44	1 15	2 43	4 40	6 6	6 45	11 19		E—Stops when required to take up passengers for Aylesbury, Harrow or London on notice being given at the station.
Whetstone	6 49		8 34	9 39		11 30	1 24		4 59		7 43	11 29		HC—Horse-boxes and carriage traffic not conveyed by these trains.
Ashby Magna	6 55		8 43	9 45		11 39	1 33					11 36		H H—Horse-box traffic not to be conveyed between intermediate stations by this train.
Lutterworth	7 5		8 51	9 56		11 47	1 41	3 20			11 50			J—Stops when required to set down passengers for the Great Western or Metropolitan lines.
Rugby	7 15	8 40	9 12	10 6	11 5	1 51	3 40		6 35	6 45	E 1 30			R—Stops on Saturdays only when required to take up passengers for London on notice being given at the station.
Willoughby	7 26		9 9	10 14		12 5	1 59			6 53				S—Stops when required to take up first-class passengers for London on notice being given at the station.
Charlwelton			9 21	10 26		12 17	2 11			7 5				
Stratford-on-Avon		8 10		9 50		12 35			6 0					Wednesdays and Saturdays only.
Fenny Compton			9 24											
Byfield			9 39											
Woodford	7 45	8 57	9 37	10 31		1 27	2 37	4 0	6 55	7 10				
Culworth			9 33				2 23			7 17				
Helmdon	7 58		9 42				2 31			7 24				
Brackley	8 10	9 50	10 44	11 48		1 41	2 37	4 15		7 31				
Finmere	8 19		9 57				2 45	4 22		7 40				
Calvert	8 36		10 13	E			2 55			7 49				
Aylesbury	8 51	10 33	11 11	12 44		2 67	3 49	4 48	J	8 10				
Harrow	9 32	11 16	11 51	12 54				5 25		8 51				
London (Marylebone)	9 50	10 20	11 32	12 5	1 10	3 0	4 20	5 43	6 40	8 2	9 15	3 25		

113

Culworth

The village itself was served by two Great Central stations, Culworth and Eydon Road halt, both of which were early casualties of closure. In actual fact, Eydon Road was closer to the village than Culworth station by some three-and-a-half miles.

end of 1919 there was a massive influx of locomotives, some 220, awaiting repair at Gorton in Manchester, the main works of the Great Central. In April of that same year Sir Sam Fay left his post at the War Office.

Meanwhile railwaymen at the lower end of the pay scale were poorly paid and since they were dissatisfied with their conditions, a meeting was called in April 1919 by ASLEF to standardise wages and conditions of service. This ensured payment of a guaranteed week, annual leave and rest intervals. As a result of this improvement in conditions, other railwaymen demanded the same treatment. The government would not agree to this so the NUR struck to obtain their rights. Nine days

later the government relented and gave way to the strikers. While the railways had been on strike, however, road transport was given a unique opportunity to prove itself.

The ensuing period saw the Great Central begin to get back its former speed and efficiency, especially on the London Extension. The 'Atlantic' and 'Director' Classes were given a fair chance to boast their capabilities. In the next year the practice of 'slipping' was returned to the Great Central. The dropping off of the rear coach was an economical way of serving some of the rural stations without interfering with express workings. One traditional working was the Marylebone-Bradford express which set down a coach at Woodford Halse for Stratford-

Culworth

Looking down the main street, amidst the quaint thatched cottages, towards the road underbridge at Eydon Road, over which the Woodford–Banbury link passed.

Culworth Village.

ipon-Avon. Since its withdrawal during the First World War, another working came in prior to its reintroduction in 1921. This other service slipped at Brackley from the Marylebone-Manchester express on the viaduct to drift into the station before being worked forward to Woodford. After its first run, the Brackley slip reverted to being attached to the Bradford train until September 1921. The one coach served Helmdon which was a small village, also on the Northampton and Banbury Junction Railway and the river Tove, both of which were crossed by the viaduct north of the station. The huge embankment and cutting at either end of the platform made the Great Central a prominent feature of this sleepy village. In March

1963 Helmdon lost its last rail link, the other being closed in 1951. Goods traffic, however, lingered on until 2 November 1964.

South of Helmdon the line entered a deep cutting for three miles leading up to Brackley station, which was slightly different to the other island-platform designs because it had a side access rather than the normal central entrances, due to the fact that the local council were worried that the traffic generated by the London Extension would create congestion on the main Towcester Road.

Brackley, at the turn of the century, already had its own station which was able to connect with the Great Western at Banbury and the London Midland Scottish at Verney Junction, though it was a more tor-

Helmdon
The station was one of two – the other, belonging to the London North Western, was named Helmdon Village. The village never experienced the growth which the railways expected of it.

Helmdon
The village has changed very little over the years and it is almost possible to imagine oneself back in the early days of the Great Central.

tuous route than the London Extension and only single track. Brackley Central was a small goods depot, handling coal, wool, corn and timber, which were some of the staple industries of the town. Brackley itself dates back to the Domesday Book when it was known as Brachelai or Brackele, and later its importance grew in medieval times through fairs and markets. Evidence of its early origins can be seen in the architecture of the Hospital of St John which is a twelfth-century foundation. Other buildings of note are the church of St Peter with its beautiful tower and the Magdalen College School, founded by William Wayneflete, Bishop of Winchester, in 1447. The school indeed provided the Great Central with regular custom, like Stowe did for Finmere. Like Helmdon, the line made a grand exit from Brackley over the 23-arch viaduct which crossed the river Ouse and its flood plain before disappearing into a cutting and crossing the LMS, leaving a leisurely coast in to the isolated platform at Finmere, from whence slip workings also ran. Finmere's service was introduced in 1923 and continued to work well into LNER

days. Finmere itself was scattered with wealthy commuters who, in the main, took advantage of the service in addition to the villagers. Amongst the distinguished patrons were Admiral Roger Keyes, who lived at Tingewick and was a hero of the Zeebrugge Raid; Captain Ferrass Loftus from Tingewick Hall; the Honourable L. Fleischmann, a banker from Chetwode Manor; and Charles William Trotter who had taken up a post as Director of the London North Eastern Railway and he lived at the beautiful Barton Hartshorn Manor. These prominent figures were undoubtedly the reason behind the choice of Finmere as a slipping venue. A bonus for the Great Central was the opening of the school at Stowe, which was a short distance away across the fields, providing a useful form of transportation for staff and pupils alike, not forgetting the revenue returns for the railway. The slip coach was worked forward to Woodford after setting down at Finmere.

The last island platform along the Great Central's London Extension was Calvert which lay to the south of the main Oxford-

Brackley Central
The opening of a major new railway provided an excuse for a holiday, feasting and many other celebrations. The enthusiasm of the town is displayed by the crowds of people and dignitaries watching the first train draw in, a far cry from the turnout at closure some 67 years later.

Brackley Central

Taken from the north end of the station, this picture gives an idea of the size of the complex. The building on the right is the entrance hall and general store and, by the looks of it, the bike shed. In the background one can just make out the goods shed and two trains, one of vans and another carrying lorries. The tower behind the footbridge and staircase belongs to the lift shaft which was used for transferring heavy loads to the platform level. Lifts were provided at Loughborough and Nottingham Victoria. At the end of the station is the signal box.

Brackley Central

Driver and fireman take a well-earned break as No. 45493 waits at Brackley Central. The island platform was a typical feature of the Great Central. The footbridge had to be provided because the station access was not permitted to be gained from the road as it was feared that traffic congestion would be caused, so the entrance hall was built in a lay-by to the left of the picture. The space in the foreground was once occupied by a siding.

Finmere
The station building, which proudly proclaims on its signboard 'Finmere for Buckingham'. The actual platform itself was entered from the road below, which led to the village two miles away. The title 'Buckingham' was used to try to woo passengers away from using the rival London and North Western Railway.

Cambridge which crossed at Claydon. Calvert had originally consisted of just one or two houses and a farm, and was not even recognised as a village. The derivation of the name is indeed interesting as it stems from the Verney family who were the local landowners. Sir Harry Verney had been born a Calvert by marriage and after he had inherited the family estate at Claydon he became a Verney. He was for many years MP for Buckingham and at the time of his marriage he began to develop a growing interest in railways and by the time the Great Central had arrived in 1899 he had decided to dedicate a station to the memory of his mother. In later years Calvert developed an industry producing bricks. This brought the need for housing for the workers and as a result a small settlement grew up there. Apart from bricks, Calvert goods yards dealt with the usual commoditites such as coal, timber, milk, etc.

Two-and-a-half miles to the south of Calvert lay Grendon Underwood Junction where the line split into two. One portion reached Marylebone via High Wycombe, while the other went via Amersham. There were two stations along this route: one at Akeman Street and the other at Wotton, where the staionmaster also looked after the nearby tramway station until it was closed

down. The Grendon-Ashendon Junction was a relief line like the Woodford-Banbury link.

By the summer of 1921 almost all pre-war cross-country services which relied on the Woodford-Banbury line were reinstated, except the route to and from Dover. One of the main features of the GC had been its development of through lines and carriages. It has also been part of the longest continuous route from Aberdeen to Penzance, a distance of 792 miles. The service which took approximately twenty-two hours began on 3 October; stops included Edinburgh (Waverly), Newcastle on Tyne, York, Sheffield (Victoria), Leicester Central, Banbury, Oxford, Swindon, Exeter, Torquay and Plymouth. At Swindon the through coaches were attached to a GWR express sleeper service to Penzance. Three additional services were instituted in the summer: (1) a dining car train between Sheffield and Oxford, Bath and Bristol and (2) & (3) restaurant cars between Mansfield and London, and between Liverpool and Lowestoft.

On 9 August 1922, the GC War Memorial was unveiled by Field Marshal Earl Haig. Special trains brought relatives and friends of the GC employees who had fallen in the First World War. The engine *Earl Haig* hauled an ordinary train from Marylebone, to which the

Calvert

The last island platform on the Great Central was set amidst rolling fields and was provided with the usual lavish goods facilities. The few houses which went to make up the village were close to the station and brickworks which was the major source of employment in the area. In the foreground a train of empty mineral wagons for the brickworks sits in the siding near the signal cabin. The date is probably the mid-thirties to judge from the London North Eastern Railway Company advertisements on the walls of the ticket office.

Calvert Cabin

Taken around the time of construction, the picture shows the signalman posing for Sydney Newton's camera. This is a somewhat earlier picture than the previous one, as the siding has not yet been extended and the trees to the right of the signal box were later cut down to put up the power lines.

Director's saloon was attached for the use of the Field Marshal himself, the Chairman and Directors and General Manager of the GC. The simple memorial was dedicated and wreaths laid on behalf of the GC Board.

The year 1922 was outstanding for the GC for a number of projects. Bays were constructed in the pier at New Holland and part of the fish market at Grimsby was rebuilt. Also preparations put in hand for the British Empire Exhibition at Wembley, which involved a new siding, loop-line station and resignalling work between Marylebone and Neasden. An important innovation in the latter project was the installation of automatic three aspect colour light signalling: this was the first use of the system in main-line operation. To suit this the Reliostop mechanical brake control employed on this section of the line had to be adapted. Equally important was the installation of remote control of points at Quainton Road. Track circuits and electrically-operated points allowed the junction to be controlled from Quainton Road signal box from early on in 1923: the GC-Metropolitan signal box was dispensed with.

In 1922 a Ministry of Transport Bill, which had occupied both the Houses of Lords and Commons for five-and-a-half months, was finally passed without any consultation

Quainton Road

A busy scene at Quainton, taken in the early 1900s just after the opening of the Great Central. The junction with the London Extension and signal box can be seen framed in the main arch of the roadbridge. The rather unusual signals follow the design of an early Metropolitan pattern. The Aylesbury train is probably due, as platform 1 has quite a large number of passengers waiting in fine Victorian dress, while the Verney Junction side seems to be doing very little business. Note the small billboard on the station wall for the Great Central, as opposed to the three provided for the Metropolitan.

with the railway companies, who were not informed of its provisions. Sir Eric Geddes was appointed the first Minister of Transport: this was the beginning of the plan to make 140 companies into four major companies, namely the GWR, LMSR, LNER and SR. Plans for the scheme by which this would be effected were drawn up in a circular dated 3 August 1922. Messrs Faringdon, Gair, Beazley, Butler and Henderson were elected to serve on the LNER Board, at a meeting in Manchester on 17 November. It was then agreed that Directors who were to become redundant should be compensated with a golden handshake of £20,000 and that the GC should cease independent operation on 31 December 1922, being thereafter under the jurisdiction of the LNER. The last GC Directors' meeting was called on 15 December to decide how to pay off the Chairman and Deputy Chairman. Sir Sam Fay was retained in an advisory capacity for the LNER, with an annual salary of £2,000. By the end of 1922 the GC owned 531 miles of track, an additional 89¼ miles of joint line, 60 miles leased and 74 miles jointly leased. Including sidings and other

track it owned a total of 2,698¾ miles. Its capital issued of preferred and deferred stock amounted to £55,089,216. The table opposite relates to receipts for 1923:

The GC thus became part of the LNER which was the second largest group, whose mileage was only exceeded by that of the LMS. The LNER empire included other companies like the Great Northern and Great Eastern, both of which had close connections with the GC.

As has been observed, the war left its mark on the railways which had suffered from the depletion of rolling stock and, to some extent, from enemy action. After the war a sound maintenance programme was much needed. The small companies, however, were in serious financial difficulties and the situation had been made worse by government policy which froze railway rates and charges linking them to wages and prices. The result of this was that Britain's railways were working with a loss of no less than £45,000,000 a year by 1920-21. There were two possibilities for lowering the deficit and restoring the system. The one was 'nationalisation' with overall government control – an expedient

	Gross receipts £	Expenditure £	Net receipts £
Railway	10,964,821	8,880,403	2,084,418
Steamship	265,698	251,346	14,352
Canals	13,398	35,651	Dr 22,253
Docks, harbours and wharves	378,358	312,877	65,481
Hotels, refreshment rooms and restaurant cars	252,495	235,341	17,154
	11,874,770	9,715,618	2,159,152
Miscellaneous receipts (net)			204,152
	11,874,770	9,715,618	2,363,304

Quainton Road
Little F7 2-4-2 tank 8307 stands at the platform for Aylesbury with the 3.30pm ex Verney Junction in the last year of operation. This particular service was operated on a push-pull basis.

rejected out of hand; the other plan involved the creation of four major, economically viable, companies from the 140 small private independent companies.

In 1923 amalgamation provided a useful support for a system of private enterprise, which in the long run did not really achieve its objective in recreating the prosperous industry that the railways once were. Many people realise now that it was perhaps a gross error on the part of the government not to have nationalised the railways in 1923. The railways recovered very little in the post-war period since they had never been permitted to have a free hand in raising costs. In 1921 a tribunal was set up to discuss railway rates and it was agreed that only standard charges could be raised, meaning that it would merely be possible to collect a standard revenue which would match profits achieved in 1913.

Due to the general trade depression and the growth of competition from road transport, no actual profit was made. The financial situation was always very tight. The LNER had the worst record for payment on ordinary dividends and stocks and shares; not one of their first or second preference shares was paid in full or regularly, while ordinary preference shareholders never obtained a penny after 1930. The LNER would have had difficulty in raising capital for any venture both before and after the Second World War. However, it showed its major wounds in the slump. Even if the company had sufficient capital, it is scarcely credible that such a large private venture could have succeeded in financing itself.

A dilemma such as the latter also prevented the London North Eastern railway from achieving any modernisation programme they wished to embark upon. The LNER adopted a cautious approach but they had nevertheless taken a lead in introducing express freights and streamlined engines. No progress

Upper South Junction
An 0-6-0 J11 works past the junction with the Verney Junction line, with an 'up' mixed freight. On the right can be seen the tracks of the old line to Verney which, by this stage, had long since been out of use.

had been made as yet in the removal of the number one evil of the railway system – namely the unbraked wagon. In terms of modernisation and improvement, the GWR and LNER put their trust in electrification but needless to say they never had the right amount of capital to embark upon a project of this nature.

Meanwhile the London Extension was surviving reasonably well as a main line. There had been some question as to what should be done with the GC since its lines crossed two territories, while the London main line really entered Midland territory at Nottingham, Leicester and Sheffield. This same problem was later to cause the demise of the line after nationalisation in 1947. For the LNER the GC showed itself to be a slight millstone, although it did provide an adequate standby route for cheap services between London and the North East.

For the London Extension the years 1935-45 were eventful in a number of ways. On 2 December 1935, after a struggle to compete with motor lorry traffic, the Brill branch from Quainton Road dropped out of the network: this was a significant omen for the future.

From 6 July 1936, the Metropolitan and LNER withdrew passenger trains and terminated them at Aylesbury. The freight link with Verney Junction lingered on until

1940, when one track was taken out of use while the other followed into disuse as the war progressed, (the junction at Quainton Road was removed in 1946). In turn Winslow Road, Granborough Road and Waddesdon Manor stations were closed.

In February 1936 another feature of the line came to an end: this was the slip coach which had been in an accident a few months previously. The accident had occurred at Woodford and was caused by a malfunction of the vacuum brake on the main train, which caused a collision between it and the slip coach. Had the train been equipped with the Robinson anti-telescoping device, this accident might never have happened. It proved that slip coaches were vulnerable and so the LNER abandoned their use for fear of a similar accident.

In the last years of the thirties war became more and more likely as the Germans continued to mobilise. The parades at the Munich Olympic games of 1936 were an indication of the future intentions of the Reich. By 1937 the government and railway directors were already planning for a full-scale emergency. The terrifying prospect of air raids was envisaged and various schemes were devised to counter this threat: evacuation and civil defence measures were planned with the railways in view. Also their use in military supplies was discussed. The railways were prepared. With the outbreak of war imminent, the government took over the groups and the then LPTB as well as some other minor companies, in the form of a Railway Executive committee. The REC was chaired by Sir Ralph Wedgewood, chairman of the LNER. The Committee was based in the old Down Street underground station on the Piccadilly line (this was also the office for Winston Churchill). In the first week of September 1939 the four companies moved into secret locations outside London.

In the first few days of September one of the most incredible mass passenger transportation schemes was put into operation – the evacuation of some 600,000 persons (mostly children) from London and another 700,000 from other cities in England and Scotland.

On the GC the number of services was drastically reduced and slowed down. A speed limit of 60mph was enforced nationwide for the duration of the war. There was a plan, however, to increase services to provide holiday trains for Whitsuntide. These plans had to be abandoned when the Germans invaded the Low Countries and Dunkirk was evacuated. More than 300,000 soldiers were moved back to London by 565 specials: another 200 specials carried survivors to Plymouth from the coast.

The movement of goods and freight did not keep pace with the demand for transportation because, while they steadily increased, until 1943, the construction of new rolling-stock was limited and there were few repair shops. Also there was a need for a more efficient loading system. The actual percentage of freight conveyed during the years up to 1943 had maintained a steady 43% above the peacetime level. As in the First World War, the GC's workshops at Gorton were turned over to the production of munitions, arms and aircraft.

New air bases in SE England and East Anglia had to be manned to counter German attacks and the LNER calculated that it loaded 460 trains with men for the East Anglian bases alone.

In the run-up to D-Day some 24,459 special trains were run to transport troops, equipment and supplies. This period was undoubtedly the busiest in the GC's history: civilian specials were forbidden and the military took over control of mail and ambulance trains and also trains for carrying German PoWs. The crisis point was reached in 1944 and the railways nearly cracked under the strain. Passenger trains were overcrowded, the termini bursting at the seams.

The impact of the Second World War on the railway system was very serious. Damage due to enemy aerial attacks was further compounded by the limited replacement of rolling-stock. The financial implications were devastating and nothing short of massive subsidies would be likely to restore anything

Woodford Halse
Woodford station, looking south, showing the main island platform, Byfield and Banbury platform and footbridges. Woodford was the only station on the London Extension between Quainton and Nottingham, save for Brackley, to have a footbridge. In the background, the formation of Woodford North Junction can be seen along with No. 4 signal cabin. The greenhouse-like structure behind the water column covered the stairway leading from the road up to the ticket office. Woodford's island platform was similar to those at Rugby and Loughborough.

approaching prewar services. One further important factor was the loss of feight to road transport: this was a problem which was to grow in the post war period.

After the war companies only received half the revenue they made and had to divide this equally among themselves. Most of the traffic was carried at sub-standard rates, even government goods. The Treasury in all pocketed £176,000,000 from the railways' profit and barely compensated them for the damage they had suffered in the war. The postwar government put the railway system very low on the list of priority for investment and repair. However, a few concessions were allowed and the GC benefited from one of these – namely the Manchester-Woodhead-Sheffield electrification. Nevertheless the damage was done, since the railways should have been subsidised to allow the commencement of a complete programme of modernisation in 1945. Unfortunately, motor vehicles and lorries were already beginning to overrun the roads like a plague!

In 1945 the newly-elected Labour Party presented the Bill for Nationalisation which not sur-prisingly was rejected by the Big Four who were unwilling to countenance the idea of such a takeover. With the imminence of state control of the railway network, many of the chief officers of the companies declined offers from the government and settled for early retirement. Others, however, greeted the introduction of nationalisation and the development of the British Transport Commission as the salvation of the railways. But was it?

The First of January 1948, known as 'Railway Sunday', saw the end of the Big Four companies and also of the London Passenger Transport Board. The railways came under regional control with the headquarters of the system in London. The fundamental reason for the creation of a state-controlled system was to institute a Transport Commission which would act on the wishes of the people and build a more efficient, integrated service with the road network, thus ensuring that the best mode of transportation might be provided for all kinds of traffic.

The two regions which were associated with the Great Central, namely the Eastern and the London

Woodford Halse loco
On 10 April 1960 the shed is seen with a fine selection of engines waiting for use. On the right is B1 61078. In the middle stands an unidentified 9F, while on the left by the water column stands sister engine No. 92216. The 9Fs were the mainstay of the Woodford–Annesley 'Windcutters' and 'Runners' until their demise in 1965. The 9Fs were stationed at Annesley but were frequent visitors to Woodford shed before returning home. The two engines near the sheer legs are two of Woodfords eight K3 2-6-0s.

'East Midlander' at Woodford

46251, *City of Nottingham* (a fitting engine for the Great Central route) draws a shining set of ex LMS carriages out of the 'up' platform at Woodford Halse on a return 'East Midlander' train to London chartered by the Railway Correspondence and Travel. Of interest is the express headcode above the buffer beam and the shed plate No. 5A (Crewe North).

Woodford loco

Depot modernisation came to Woodford for a brief spell as an attempt was made to dieselise the line. Here, in this 1959 photograph, the oil storage tank and diesel shed are nearing completion. The only diesels ever to be stationed at Woodford were four BR shunters which did not make use of these facilities.

Midland, lost most of their identity in the reshuffling, because a new Scottish region was created also the Northern Eastern region which reduced the size of the former great empires.

All regions were restricted in budget and had to get approval from the Transport Commission headquarters in London before they could embark on any large-scale projects. The other restricting factor was the decision to retain steam traction when other countries were making progress in experimenting with diesel traction. The

LMS had, however, already produced two mainline diesels Nos. 10000 and 10001 which made their inaugural non-stop London-Glasgow run in 1947.

At the same time, both Southern and Western regions were carrying out experiments. The GWR tried out two gas turbine locomotives Nos. 18000 and 18100, built in Switzerland and by Metro Vickers respectively: both proved unsuccessful. Three new locomotives were assessed on the Southern, one electric (No. 20009), with a pantograph and third rail control;

Woodford Halse
One of the sadder sights at Woodford was this picture of No. 45292 working the 4.38 ex Marylebone on a 'down' train to Nottingham on the last train as the chalk markings on the smoke-box door show. At this stage the shed plate has been taken off and its home depot is crudely chalked on the buffer beam. Note the fact that the footbridge cover and the signal arms have already been removed.

a diesel electric (No. 10203) which hauled the 'Atlantic' coast express; and the ill-fated 36001 'Leader' Class (steam); all built by O. V. Bulleid. The assumption that steam was the best mode of traction was a major factor in slowing down the recovery rate of the network and hampered the development of the modernisation of British Railways. Resources were directed towards improvements in steam locomotive design, as in the case of 71000 *The Duke of Gloucester* and the 9F Class, at a time when the railways should have been introducing new and more flexible forms of traction such as diesel and electric.

A reluctance to do dirty work led to a decrease in the number of staff willing to join maintenance depots and this, together with the scarcity of coal and the fact that it was often of poor quality, led inevitably to unreliable performance in engines. Even the new designs were unable to circumvent these problems.

The British Transport Commission clearly did not achieve its aims in restoring the system and furthermore failed to check accumulating

losses sustained in operation. This led to a rift between the BTC and the railway executive which further impeded progress in postwar modernisation plans. With the return of a Conservative government under Sir Winston Churchill, railways were again in the news and there was even some talk of turning back the clock and restoring the Big Four companies. This was not, however, a serious possibility and in 1953 the Conservatives passed an Act which disbanded the railway executive and part of the BTC: each region was given a chief manager whose power and authority were correspondingly increased. Such managers negotiated directly with a railway body within the BTC.

It was not until 1955, some ten years after the war, that the BTC was finally allowed to embark on a modernisation plan backed by financial aid from the government. General Sir Brian Robertson, the newly appointed Chairman, estimated that the plan for the revitalisation of the railway network would cost £1,240,000,000, a staggering figure but one which could have been recouped by an efficient system. The main part of the plan involved traction units and rolling-stock suitable for running at speeds of 70-100mph, with electricty providing the motive power. The principal routes were to be electrified, resignalled and be provided with better track. The main lines for this treatment were Kings Cross-York, Euston-Liverpool and all lines out of Liverpool Street and Fenchurch Street. There was no mention, however, of the Marylebone-Sheffield or Great Western lines. The plan was for the Southern Region to provide third rail for the rest of the lines, which at that time were unelectrified.

For secondary routes and branch lines, the plan chose diesel traction and diesel multiple units which were intended to reduce operational losses. The most difficult task by far was the provision of new wagons which could be controlled by the locomotive – a system which would allow goods trains to

Woodford Halse
No. 44984 on the 5.15pm ex Nottingham Victoria steams out of Woodford to Marylebone with one final effort as the black smoke shows. The wreath and crowds on the platform say it all – for this is the last day.

travel at higher speeds to their respective destinations. The British railway system remained archaic compared with its foreign counterparts in the postwar era. BR retained the vacuum brake system until it was nearly too late. Indeed, modernisastion was achieved too late to regain traffic for the railways. It had been an error of judgement to assume that the country would wait until the railways had put their house in order. Road transport, combined with the increase in the number of cars on the road, caused a gradual but significant loss of business for the railways. The DMUs were only profitable on suburban routes and in cross-country operations: goods carried by the railways fell by 12% in 1958 as the then new trunk-road system began to be developed. The line worst hit by changed circumstances was the Great Central, thanks to the M1 which not only served the towns but ran alongside the line at Whetstone and Ashby Magna. It lost much of its freight traffic overnight, especially refrigerated freight.

Rises in labour costs and the price of materials caused BR to re-appraise its plans for the future of the system. BR admitted that the BTC and the world, in general terms, were light years away from each other in reality. The economy was not expanding fast enough to allow capital to be provided for the railways. The railways, in turn, were unable to increase fares fast enough to offset wage increases. Thus it was predicted by BTC that if the modernisation programme was speeded up, then the railways would display a working surplus of £50-100 millions by 1963.

BR concentrated on three main types of diesel; the oil burner, the diesel electric and the diesel hydraulic. Most of the latter were of German design and saw service on the Western Region, but the much beloved 'Western' Class traversed the GW/GC line when they worked the Paddington-Wycombe-Birmingham expresses during the twilight years of the route. During the brief attempt to dieselise the Great Central, which never really gained any momentum, the London Extension saw a variety of the diesel electric type,

Woodford Junction
Only in times of demand such as on summer long-distance workings were 9Fs employed on passenger duties. Here, 9F 92154 is leaving Woodford Halse on a Bradford–Poole express on a fine August day in 1964. The line on the left curved away to Byfield and Stratford-upon-Avon. Note the unspoiled countryside of the Northampton uplands which lies in the the background. There is little evidence in the picture of the massive railway complex that went to make up Woodford Halse.

Diesels on the Great Central
An eight-coach Class 115 DMU in green livery, packed with rail enthusiasts, approaches Brackley on the last day, 3 September 1966. These units were employed on one or two workings a day prior to closure between Marylebone and Nottingham Victoria. Subsequently they were transferred to the Marylebone–Banbury and Marylebone–Aylesbury routes.

supplied by English Electric. The diesels, though, were confined to football specials or filling in turns and long distance workings. Elsewhere on the British railway network dieselisation was spreading rapidly and by the close of 1958 BR had 105 diesels, 2,417 DMUs and only 16,108 steam engines.

In the wake of the new form of traction came the need for new maintenance depots and fuelling facilities for diesels: there were two built on the Great Central, one at Darnall, in Sheffield, which housed a variety of diesel types employed on the York-Poole expresses; while the other, at Woodford, was provided only for the allocation of modern traction (four 350 BHP diesel shunters only were kept on shed). Even though Woodford was without the advantage of full dieselisation, the question still remains as to why this folly was allowed and what would have happened if Woodford had, in fact, become dieselised. One can only speculate, as the Great Central was not included in any modernisation plan, but a few improvements were made such as the introduction of colour-light signalling and the provision of new track and, finally, the building of a new station at Banbury to cater more easily for future traffic from the GC.

In the same year, 1958, the GC suffered another tremendous setback with the termination of its

affiliation to the Eastern Region. Instead, it became affiliated to the Midland, which had always been its rival, and the merger was effected by the drafting of new regional officials to run the line. It was not long, however, before the Midland men discovered that the GC had its own traditions and operating methods. One bone of contention lay in the loadings, or weight of trains. Thus in every respect it could be said that major changes were taking place which, with the new management and the dawning of the diesel age, meant that the railway industry was creating a totally different environment in which to work. Although conditions were easier, many employees mourned the passing of the age of steam and its excitement as one driver, who had been with the GC for forty-five years, vividly recalls in the following account.

Life in the railway company employ was, admittedly, very tough with bad conditions even for the enginemen. At sixteen you could become a call boy which entailed walking round the dark streets with no lighting, knocking on engine drivers' doors to rouse them for their shift. Call boys worked three eight-hourly shifts starting at 8am. If they were not required for call duty they cleaned the depot, or were sent to the lodging houses to do similar chores there. It was the beginning of a long drawn-out training – twenty years to reach the position of a fully-fledged engine driver.

After an initial period of three years, the trainee became a passed fireman which meant that he could be called out on any job as a relief fireman.

In 1924-5 the top pay was £4.50 for a driver. A year later, 1926, with the General Strike, work ceased from May to December. Times were very hard and it was during this period that Mr Harris, who was based at Woodford, remembers being laid off and having to camp out while walking to Banbury, where he appeared before a tribunal to put his claim for a mere 25p-a-week pay rise. In 1929-30, to keep the GC solvent and so preserve their livelihood, the railwaymen suffered a 2½% loss because of the slump. Subsequently, however, the men went on to win their fight for the meagre increase in pay.

The next stage in Mr. Harris's career was an upgrading from passed fireman to full-time fireman: this was still two stages away from being a qualified engine driver.

Drivers and firemen worked long shifts and often their duties entailed working as far as Lincoln, Manchester, York, and Sheffield, working back to Banbury loaded, having hauled an empty fish train to Grimsby. The men also went on little jobs such as the 'Weekend splash'. This entailed going to Sheffield and staying the night there in very cold dormitories. Conditions were so bad that, as Mr Harris recalled: 'We often had to use the doormats and any floor covering for additional bedclothes.' There were dormitories at Woodford, Manchester and Annesley, where drivers and firemen could obtain a meal, wash and a night's sleep. In some of these lodgings, drivers had to share accommodation with firemen, which only goes to prove that, in spite of such provisions, life was hard even for engine drivers, a privileged class in the railway hierarchy. However, dormitory facilities, spartan as they were, seemed preferable to conditions found in cheap lodging-houses!

The men were given chisels, hammers and other tools from Sheffield as 'perks'. At Christmas they received puddings and boxes of oranges. It was felt that these

Banbury Western Region
Taken from the roadbridge, this May 1962 picture shows the new and rather extensive facilities provided at Banbury which were built as part of the modernisation plan. In the background, behind the gasometer, lay Merton Street station which was the terminus of the route from Bletchley. A bay was provided for this branch in the new station as it was intended to divert trains over a new spur into the Great Western section, but this never came about as the line was closed soon after the platform was provided. On the left, in the goods yard, is a trainload of rails, while in the bay 46118 waits to take a three-coach local train to Woodford Halse. This service ceased in 1964. On the right is Great Western station pilot No. 7905 *Fowey Hall* standing in the parcels dock with a siphon wagon.

'perks' and double pay made such trips worthwhile.

After twenty years as a fireman and pass fireman (the next stage when a fireman was cleared for driving duties), the Company called together future drivers. They had then to take a tough exam and, on reaching the necessary standard, became fully-fledged drivers. The best engine drivers were those who knew the road and did not abide by the book entirely!

Below is a table showing the various stages of Mr Harris' career:

1921	Traffic Department
1923	Call Boy/Cleaner 16 years old
1926	Strike May-December
1930	Slump reduced
1926-37	Fireman
1937-43	Pass Fireman
1943-65	Driver

Looking at the above table, it took him twenty-two years to become a driver and nowadays it is possible to drive an engine after five years. The conditions are obviously better now, but one must not forget that the skill and precision required for driving a steam locomotive is far greater. Basically the railwayman had a tough training and a hard life, despite the 'perks'.

Woodford Halse Railwaymen's Social Club, now the home of the Great Central Railway Enthusiasts' Association.

Brackley Central
44872 eases its way into Brackley's island platform with the 8.15am ex Nottingham Victoria on the last day of the Great Central through workings between Marylebone and Nottingham, 3 September 1966. Note the little gathering that has assembled by the water tower.

Finmere House
Finmere House seen here from the front view in 1951. It was the residents of houses such as this, Barton Hartshorn, Chetwode, Tingwick and other dwellings in the area that encouraged the Great Central to put a station nearby. The latter was also convenient for another large institution namely Stowe School.

Opposite
V2 Class, 60961 is seen passing Quainton Road South Junction with an afternoon local train to Woodford.

Steaming Through the Chilterns

BRITISH RAILWAYS

STEAMING THROUGH
THE CHILTERNS
THE FINAL YEARS

Quainton Road was the last port of call for the London Extension before joining the Metropolitan tracks as far as Marylebone and, because it had been an established station long before the arrival of the Great Central, the station was of normal design. However, the present day site of the platforms is about eighty yards south of the station which was established by the Aylesbury & Buckingham Railway who were the predecessors of the Metropolitan in the Quainton area. The Metropolitan had extended out from Aylesbury and taken over the Wotton Tramway and the Aylesbury & Buckingham Railway in 1890, while some nine years later the Great Central took over the running rights of the latter lines. This set the scene for what was to be the busiest period throughout Quainton Road's history, as the station had trains coming and going in all directions to and from Marylebone; then there were the local services and the Wotton

Tramway line and the trains which plyed to and from the 'up' and 'down' yards. In 1904 Quainton was mainly the domain of the Metropolitan Company but the Great Central did provide a local service for passengers and horse-boxes. For both companies, however, the two world wars saw a considerable increase in traffic due to supply movements and ordinary services for the war effort. By the end of the Second World War Quainton ceased to be a junction. The tramway had been abandoned in 1935 and the branch to Verney Junction fell in July 1936, although the track was not lifted until 1946. In order to compensate for the loss of the latter, a chord was built just north of Calvert which connected with the Oxford-Bletchley line on which Verney Junction was a station. Another result of the war was the erection of a Ministry of Agriculture food buffer depot which was served by its own private siding. By 1956 the picture at Quainton was somewhat changed because the Metropolitan had been cut back to Aylesbury, and British Rail provided the sole local service until the station was closed in 1963, when all local stations north of

Aylesbury Town
Two days before the end of services north of Aylesbury, 44840, one of the last engines stationed at the now-closed Woodford Halse shed, waits in platform 3 to take the 4.38pm ex Marylebone–Nottingham. Whilst the engine is being watered the driver and fireman are deep in conference, probably about the future of the line. In the background is the goods yard and coal depot.

Aylesbury Town

A resplendent station plays host to 44858 on the 5.15pm 'up' express ex Nottingham Victoria. The train boasts a full load with eight coaches even at this late stage. The carriages are comprised of British Rail Mk1 stock. On the right the new order stands in the sidings in the form of a diesel multiple unit which are used on the Aylesbury and Banbury–Marylebone diagrams.

Aylesbury Town

With ease, V2 60817 pounds away from the station towards Brackley with a Leicester express. This particular V2 was noted for being fitted with a double chimney. The stock is made up of Gresleys, with the second vehicle being painted in blood-and-custard livery. The date is 1950.

Aylesbury Town

Looking south on the right is platform 4, the platform used by Princes Risborough and Marylebone trains travelling via the Wycombe route. The point off to the right in the foreground led into the locomotive depot, which ended its days in 1968. Waiting at platform 3 is a rather grimy 44840 with the 4.38pm ex Marylebone–Nottingham Victoria. The loco is carrying the express headcode above the buffer beams.

Aylesbury South
Passing south junction and signal box juntion for Princes Risborough, 44840 approaches Aylesbury from London from the Amersham lines with the 4.38pm 'down' train to Nottingham. During the last six years the 5MT 'Stanier' Class locomotives were the mainstay of the depleted service on the London Extension.

Wendover
On a fine summer's day experimental locomotive GT3 looking very much like a cross between a diesel and a 7F, makes short work of Dutchlands Summit with its train of Mk1 stock. Powered by gas turbines, the loco made regular runs between Marylebone and Nottingham in the years 1960 and 1961, until it was withdrawn for scrap.

Aylesbury suffered the same fate: however, the yards continued to handle goods for local merchants until July 1966, a few months before the closure of the main line itself. The yard also provided a holding area for trains awaiting a path along the line to Marylebone.

One of the disadvantages of the station at Quainton was its distance from the village, which was at the top of a hill in an idyllic setting. This was a typical English village complete with olde worlde houses and a windmill which today has lost all its sails. Local inhabitants

were not too concerned about the possibility of Quainton becoming the 'Clapham Junction of the Met', as John Betjemen put it, and this is borne out by the fact that the village has changed very little since the time when the railways were experiencing their boom period.

After Quainton the next station was Aylesbury, the county town of Buckinghamshire, which has a population of some 30,000. Sadly, many of its old houses were destroyed at about the same time as the passing of the GC and the town is now a typical example of twentieth-century architecture, with modern shopping precincts and glass-faced office blocks: its council offices are a blot on the landscape. The main industries are printing, engineering, food and, to a certain extent, 'ducks'. Around the market place, a few of the old houses remain and, indeed, some of the fine old hostelries retain much of their original charm. One such inn is the Bell, now a Trust-house Forte hotel. Next door is the courthouse which has a link with railways in that it was the scene of the Great Train Robbers' trial. The other large town on the GC/GW line was High Wycombe, noted for its furniture manufacture and known also for its connections with Disraeli and the Hell Fire Club at West Wycombe Park. Its population is about 60,000 and, like Aylesbury, is an engineering and furniture making orientated town, with a modern shopping precinct, the Octagon. Also of octagonal design is the Guildhall, raised on arches and surmounted by an ornate cupola.

Beyond Aylesbury the line enters suburbia and commuter land on both the Wycombe and Amersham routes to Marylebone, its final destination. The set-up is totally different from the poorly patronised stations on the local runs north of Aylesbury town. The

prophetic utterance made in earlier years by critics who believed that the Great Central was an economically unsound proposition and that it stood for 'Gone Completely', became only too true in the sixties. Perhaps the most important reason for the failure of the GC was that its route, from the outset, was dictated by the existence of other long-established main-line routes into London. Unlike its successful rivals, the GC passed through few large towns from Nottingham (Victoria) to Marylebone.

In 1923, after only twenty-three years of operation, the GC became the LNER, although some vestiges of GC traditions lingered on: it

Great Missenden

45608 *Gibraltar* thunders through Great Missenden on an express parcels for Marylebone in September 1963. The engine is performing well, almost as if the effort is being made for the cameraman. A few alterations have been made to the station to accommodate longer trains and on the 'down' platform this necessitated the rather curious alteration to the water tower. On the right is the coal yard and sidings.

Great Missenden

67749 L1 Class pulls away from Missenden with a six-coach local train to Marylebone, passing 30719 waiting to work the *William Penn* to Waterloo on 15 May 1955. This was the first and only occasion that a member of the 'Drummond' Class visited Great Missenden. Note the decorative headboard on the smokebox door.

Amersham South End
46163 ambles out of platform 1 with a fairly light load on the 9.15am from Nottingham to Marylebone. By the time this picture was taken the electric trains had been running for two years. Even at this late stage the goods yard is still busy with freight traffic.

finally lost its identity at nationalisation. When the parent company was absorbed by BR, and the former GC came under the control of two regions: the Eastern and the Midland, the whole railway network had begun to suffer the effects of insufficient modernisation and investment in the industry. The 1960s saw the beginning of a large programme to rescue the system, directed by Dr (later Lord) Beeching who reduced the number of unprofitable branch lines in order to provide, it was hoped, a smaller, more efficient network. The effects of the Beeching 'axe' were drastic.

The London Extension had seen two named trains in its heyday, 'The Master Cutler' and 'The South Yorkshireman'. The change in regional status of the former GC/LNER to LMS affected work patterns and the efficiency of services. More and more men were made redundant and since the line was bypassed by modernisation, its death warrant had virtually been signed. It remained steam long after the dieselisation and became a line for surplus locomotives during the final years. Some restrictions on

Amersham
61028 *Umseke* at Amersham with the 10.00am Marylebone–Manchester express in April 1955. The train is fairly heavily loaded with a mixture of Gresley and British Rail Mk1 coaches. This picture was taken five years before Amersham became the terminus for London Transport Electric Trains. Note the Metropolitan and Great Central signal cabin behind the engine.

Chesham
On 11 September 1960 the London Transport Chesham Shuttle waits at Chesham to depart for the very last time. The locomotive on this train was British Railways 2-6-2T No. 41284. Seen at the head of the push-pull set, composed of Ashbury coaches, it is facing Chalfont & Latimer, the other terminus of this short, windy branch. As on many other 'trips for the last time', the train was well filled on every journey.

Chalfont & Latimer
57416, having wound its way through the wooded countryside of Chesham and Amersham, is seen here drawing into Chalfont & Latimer station with its train of London Transport stock on 26 January 1958. The train in the background is probably an express for London Marylebone.

running had been imposed in the Nottingham area due to the increase in coal mining and this had lengthened the journey time. On the 2 January 1960, express services were curtailed and the trains which ran on that fateful day showed signs of neglect and reflected the general rundown. The engines included B1s, V2s Class 5s 2-6-2 and 9Fs. The 9F locomotives had been drafted in to replace the V2s most of which had been transferred to the Eastern Region. The remaining V2s posed problems as it became difficult for the GC men to obtain spare parts from the Eastern Region when it ceased to be their parent region. This situation precipitated the run down of the line.

Between 1960 and 1961, following the world wide trend away from steam-based traction, the English Electric Company at Whetstone made a fresh start on the construction of a gas turbine locomotive which was capable of being used with many of the standard features of British Railways designs. In December 1960, after successful tests at the locomotive testing station at Rugby the previous year, the complete structure was rolled into the paint shop. By the first week of 1961, GT3, as the locomotive was known, rolled out of the works ready for main-line running.

The gas turbine was enclosed under a rectangular hood and its exhaust was carried off through two holes in the roof. There were also two large grilles containing filters and above these an exhaust for the ejector and oil cooler. The splashers covered up the large battery racks and above the buffer beam there was a fan housing. Inside, the cabin was carpeted and there was a generous amount of space. One of the advantages was

that the chassis was standard for the underframe and the tender was similar to that used on ordinary steam engines while incorporating many extra facilities. The locomotive itself was finished in a super chocolate-brown colour with orange bands.

By 1963 Lord Beeching was well established with BR, carrying through the same plans as he had with ICI, of which he had previously been Chairman. BR was making heavy losses, largely the result of a badly-timed modernisation plan. Beeching and the new BR Board, in Spring 1963, implemented a Reshaping Report to remove unprofitable lines and stations. However, the system still had

Doubleheader
K3 61809 and 5Mt 'Stanier' crawl along the grade over electrified tracks at Moor Park with a rake of Gresley and British Rail Mk1 coaches. The third vehicle is painted in the blood-and-custard livery while the rest of the train is in lined maroon livery. The date is August 1959, a year before the end of express working, and here the engines are employed on the 11.30pm Nottingham–Marylebone working. At this stage the electric rails only reached as far as Rickmansworth, where a change to steam was necessary for the journey to Aylesbury.

Beeching plans to axe a main line

By BERNARD JORDAN

PARTS of the old Great Central Railway line between Marylebone, London and Sheffield are to be scheduled for closure by Dr. Beeching.

If the plan goes through passengers between ten stations over 61 miles of main line will lose their trains.

About 1,500 railwaymen will also lose their jobs or be asked to take alternative work and industrialists will lose freight routes.

I understand the cuts, to be announced today, will be :

From Calvert North junction, Buckinghamshire, to Rugby (34 miles) ; Bulwell Common to Annesley junction, near Nottingham (61 miles) ; Kirkby Colliery to Duckmanton junction (11 miles) ; Staveley Central to Renishaw (two miles).

A branch line between Culworth junction and Banbury (eight miles) is also in the axing plan.

Main-line stations on the Great Central would not be closed but would stay open to serve other regions.

British Railways say the line is little used and their new, fast express trains link the towns on alternative routes.

Dr. Beeching's proposed cuts north of Nottingham affect freight routes only. He will ask industrialists to use alternative routes on Eastern and Midland Region tracks.

Other routes

A railways spokesman said "On the eight-mile Banbury stretch we ran only about three trains a day. And we found that not more than 20 people used any one of them.

"At the moment we only run about three through trains to Nottingham on the old Great Central Line and there are plenty of trains on other routes."

The Prime Minister and his Transport Minister, Mr. Tom Fraser, are committed by their pre-election pledges to stay the Beeching axe until they have had a full investigation of all forms of transport.

● The National Union of Railwaymen executive decide yesterday "to seek an improvement" in the 3 p.c. pay offer from the British Railways Board in reply to their 13 p.c. claim.

Their leader, Mr. Sidney Greene, said : "We have not rejected the offer. We do not like the word rejection."

Now the N.U.R. is seeking a meeting with Dr. Beeching.

What the axe means to village—Page SEVENTEEN.

What the axe means to village—Page SEVENTEEN.

Government blamed for 'death' of rail line

THE Government is deliberately "killing" the efficiency of the old Great Central rail line to provide an excuse for closing it down, claimed the South Northants Labour candidate on Sunday.

Speaking at a Woodford Halse meeting, Mr. Ivor Wilde said, "The line is running at a loss because it has been starved of traffic so that death could be made easier."

The purpose of the meeting, held in the Railwaymen's Club was to discuss the proposed withdrawal of stopping passenger trains between Marylebone and Sheffield and the possible complete closure of the old Great Central Line.

All three South Northants candidates addressed the meeting, comprised mainly of railwaymen.

Governments blamed

Said Mr. Noel Picarda, Liberal, "The workers are the experts and know how to make the profits—not Dr. Beeching."

But he blamed the governments over the past 30 years for not evolving a "coherent redundancy policy."

Conservative candidate Mr. Arthur Jones pointed out that compensation for redundant staff had been discussed.

"I am quite sure the qualifications you have gained in the railways will qualify you for jobs in other industries."

Brackley competitor Mrs. R. T. Whiteley, gained third place in the working hunter class at the British Timken Show with Little Mush on Saturday.

---

spare capacity on the trunk routes and on secondary ones. It can be argued in retrospect that the Beeching Report did more harm than good, since by destroying the supply routes to the main lines much of the railways' economy was placed in jeopardy: many of the routes had been the means of moving heavy freight. The removal of small goods depots angered local merchants who did not wish to lose their facilities, but the age of the concentration depot had inexorably arrived. As a result of such closures and the reduction in services for the public, passengers turned to travelling by road. Freight was similarly redirected. Beeching pressed on with the drastic pruning of workshops, depots and stations: staff were made redundant. Although the losses were reduced, however, the measures were not enough to prevent the implementation of a Second Report which aimed at rationalising the trunk routes as well. This plan was the 'keep or close' option, shifting duplicate main lines and unnecessary sidings. The GC was directly afffected. Local services suffered, with the closure of several small stations along the line. These local services had depended for their revenue on larger centres like Aylesbury, Rugby, Nottingham, Leicester and, of course, London itself. Between the cities of Nottingham and Leicester, twelve trains a day ran in each direction. A few of these trains, instead of acting as a shuttle service, became long-distance stopping trains. Other local trains ran between Nottingham

and Rugby, Nottingham and Woodford, Sheffield and Leicester. South of Leicester, services from Leicester-Woodford, Leicester-Rugby and Woodford-Marylebone completed the pattern. In 1963 a report was made on the Great Central to support the Beeching proposals for the reshaping of British Rail.

In March 1963 all local trains between Aylesbury and Rugby, Banbury and Woodford and Nottingham and Sheffield, including the loop at Chesterfield, were withdrawn. The end of these services meant the closure of stations at Quainton, Calvert, Finmere, Helmdon, Culworth and Braunston. The only stations to remain open on the Aylesbury-Rugby section were Woodford and Brackley. Beyond Rugby Central, a dieselised commuter service continued until the closure of the line, as far as Nottingham Victoria.

During the period 1963-4, the GC actually had an increase in traffic while the electrification of the line out of Euston was in progress. These additional trains generally ran at night and used the Calvert spur to join the Oxford-Cambridge line as far as Bletchley, where they rejoined the west coast main line. These trains ran to Crewe and Preston while the GC trains ran from York-Banbury and from Nottingham-Marylebone.

In 1964 the modest four-road engine shed at Leicester, built to accommodate 15-20 engines under cover, was closed. The sidings contained a manually operated turntable and coaling plant. It was, however, unusual to have a depot

Wembley stadium
L1 2-6-4T 67787 leaves the stadium loop with an empty train for Neasden carriage sidings. This particular corner of London was overrun with the tracks of two massive depots for the Great Central and London Transport; in fact the area was a railway colony. The sidings have all gone now as the Great Central depot was demolished and, indeed, so has the stadium loop which played host to many cup final trains and other special workings. In Great Central and LNER days these trains carried a St. Andrew's cross above one of the buffer beams.

Chesham 'The Yard'
67420 sporting a 'Lion and wheel emblem' stands at Chesham coal stage on 2 September 1950. The station, like so many other local wayside depots, boasted a very busy goods yard, especially where coal handling was concerned.

WORKERS OPPOSE RAIL CLOSURE

MORE than 80 objections have already been made to the proposed closure of the Woodford Halse-Banbury railway line.

The closure, planned for November 3rd, but postponed following the objections, would involve the withdrawal of 10 passenger trains daily, two of which carry about 80 workers to Banbury.

This was revealed on Tuesday by Mr. C. R. Fenton, clerk to Woodford Halse Parish Council, who told the "Advertiser" that he was expecting a total of between 150 and 200 letters of objection before the weekend.

Mr. Fenton said that before sending the letters to the East Midlands Transport Users Consultative Committee points would be taken from them on which the official parish council objection would be formulated.

One of the most recent letters to arrive is from a man who has to visit his wife in a Banbury hospital every day during the specified visiting hours.

This can be done easily by train, but if he had to travel by bus it would mean leaving Woodford about 8 a.m. and not returning until 6 p.m." he said.

NO ALTERNATIVE

Ald. J. W. Anscomb, chairman of both the parish council and Daventry Rural District Council, told an "Advertiser" reporter that it was hoped an approach would be made to the county council for assistance, which may include legal representation for the parish council at any public inquiry.

Mr. W. J. Preece, another Woodford Halse representative on the R.D.C., said on Tuesday that residents were concerned with the effect the closure would have on local social services.

"We rely on Banbury for hospital, maternity and dental services," said Mr. Preece. Several firms in Banbury, together with the local Chamber of Commerce, had so far agreed to support the objections.

Mr. T. Hinton, who travels by train from Woodford to Banbury daily, complained to a reporter that 'there was no adequate bus services. Six-teen-year-old Miss Edwina Smith commented, " I shall lose an hour's pay each day if the trains are stopped."

Miss Margaret Hancock, 26 Percy Road, Woodford Halse, complained of lost time and increased bus fares.

A spokesman for the Transport Users Consultative Committee in Derby said on Tuesday that the committee would consider objections after the closing date of September 20th. It was anticipated that a public meeting would be arranged in the Woodford Halse district.

where there were no junctions or terminals and Leicester had depended on the standard of its main-line performance to avert closure.

In 1965 the GC route lost all its express freight and parcels traffic except for the Nottingham-Neasden parcels train. However, from the beginning the GC had never been primarily a passenger-carrying railway because it ran through a very sparsely populated area. The freight service from Annesley-Woodford in the last years confirms this. The trains conveyed two main items, coal and steel, as well as general goods. The coal came from South Yorkshire and Nottinghamshire collieries to Annesley, where it was concentrated before being despatched to Woodford. From Woodford it was transferred to the Western Region. Steel came on low loaders from Consett, in Durham, and Scunthorpe to Annesley whence it was sent to South Wales on the

old Stratford & Midland Junction Railway which branched off to the south of Woodford station.

The Annesley-Woodford service began in 1947 and was an immediate success because trains ran non-stop between the yards, making it possible for an average of forty trains to work in each direction. In the 1960s, for the last five years of the GC, the freight trains were worked by BR standard 9F engines which formed the backbone of GC working. The Annesley-Woodford freight trains were given the name 'Runners', or 'Winductters' which was appropriate owing to their speed and efficiency which was not matched by services on other regions.

As far as modernisation went on the GC, this was limited to some of the semi-fast services being reduced to four-car diesel multiple units and a brief attempt at complete dieselisation which

Near Northwood
Taken from the front of a DMU on an 'up' local to Marylebone, a rather sad looking engine 44835 is seen here on a 'down' Nottingham train on 30 April 1966, a few months before the end of all long-distance trains.

Marylebone

44846 and 44688 stand at Marylebone coaling stage with another 'Black Five', waiting their turn of duty. Note the mechanical coaling plant which is feeding 44846, while 44688 lets off a huge cloud of smoke. In the background can be seen the many terraced houses which go to make up the area known as the parish of Marylebone. Under the bridge, at the rear of the picture, lay the beginning of the station platforms and a 70-foot turntable.

might have saved the line. This was, however, all too late and plans were abandoned. Even Woodford had some improvements in the form of a new coaling plant with an automatic tippler: the new oil depot was, in fact, never used. Four diesel shunters were also allocated to the Woodford shed where they remained until the closure.

Without the benefit of any serious attempt attempt at modernisation and the reshuffling of steam loco-motives, the GC was beset by breakdowns owing to the lack of proper facilities for maintenance. There were also minor accidents, exacerbated by excessively long signal blocks and the fact that engines could not be changed at suitable stages.

In 1965 the GC lost its freight services and this forshadowed the inevitable fate of the line. In the same year the Annesley shed was closed and its role taken over by nearby Colwick. The final straw came for Woodford when the last train left its yard. In the early hours of 4 September 1966 the

GC ceased operation as a trunk line. The repercussions for the population of Woodford were serious since the railway had been the main means of livelihood: the town was never to recover.

On the previous afternoon there was no official send-off for the GC except for the addition of extra coaches to the semi-fast trains and a special LCGB rail tour to mark the end of Watkin's dream. The train was hauled from Waterloo to Sheffield and back by Southern rebuilt Merchant Navy Class No. 35030 *Elder Dempster Lines*. Thousands turned out that final Saturday to watch and record the end of an era of a main line which had so often been on the verge of disaster. The engines which worked the last services were in very poor shape and this seemed to reduce the enthusiasm for steam traction. One engine on the Nottingham-Marylebone run flaked out at Aylesbury leaving a diesel to complete its turn.

The withdrawal of long-distance trains involved the transfer of comparatively few services to other

High Wycombe

On a glorious summer evening the 'Master Cutler' wends its way at a pace past Wycombe middle signal cabin and the massive retaining wall, on the way to delightful Chilterns countryside. The train with its rake of blood-and-custard coaches would travel through Princes Risborough and up to Ashendon Junction, where it would leave to join the link line to Grendon Underwood at which point it met up with the main line to Nottingham.

Rugby reflections

The RCTS organised many tours on the Great Central in the last six years of its existence in the shape of a train called the 'East Midlander' which always proved to be very popular. Here Midland 'Compound' No. 1000 drifts into Rugby to greet the expectant crowd of onlookers. The date is 11 September 1960.

RAIL SHUTDOWN PLAN WOULD KILL THE TOWN

THE SMALL railway town of Woodford Halse (population about 3,500), is preparing for a funeral . . . its own.

The townspeople, whose lives are bound up with the Great Central line, were stunned last week when they learned that it was next on the list for the Beeching chop.

But they will not give up without a fight. Moves are already being prepared to offer powerful opposition to a plan that could kill the town.

Mr. Charles Saunders, of Spring Cottages, Woodford,

parish clerk and railway worker, said that there were between 500 and 600 railwaymen living in the town.

"Many of them are middle aged; many of them are buying their own houses. Seventy per cent of the population depends on the railway.

"It will be very hard for people to pull up roots.

"The trades people are in a very precarious position. Everyone has been stunned by the news.

"When the line closes and the station shuts down, Woodford Halse will die."

Protests

Mr. Saunders said that his parish council, which had protested strongly when the passenger service to Banbury was withdrawn, would object to the closure of the line.

Mr. W. Preece, Northamptonshire County Councillor and president of his local branch of the A.E.U. said that Woodford had been built up around the railway.

"The town depends on the railway" he said.

The stunning effect of the announcement was reflected by his comments: "The whole thing is ridiculous. It is all so complicated, all bits and pieces.

"We are all very upset. We haven't had a chance to look at it.

Wrong age

"We are hoping that the Unions and the new Labour Government will halt it."

Mr. Jim Hancock, 51-year-old switchboard operator and timekeeper, at the doomed Woodford Halse station, is one of the many railwaymen who have settled in the town.

The prospect of moving to another job in another place, does not appeal to him.

"I am at the wrong age to get shifted," he said.

"I have seven children and I am buying my own house.

"But who will want to buy that off me. Nobody will want to come to Woodford now. There is no other industry here."

Brackley expected the axe

FOR THE people of Brackley, the axing of the station was not unexpected, and no great hardship is expected to result.

It will mean that travellers will have to catch their trains from either Bicester or Banbury.

The Borough Council is at present trying to encourage new industry to the town, as a defence against any possibility of losing its centuries-old identity as a borough.

WARNING

But no one seems to think that industrialists will be discouraged by a lack of rail facilities.

Ald. John Tweedale, the Mayor of Brackley, commented: "Not many industries use the railways anyway."

He added: "We have had plenty of warning that this might happen."

"The Council will certainly protest as we have protested before. I think the station might have been closed sometime ago, but for the Council's objections.

"I don't think it will affect the town's industry, and I don't think it will affect any new industry that comes to Brackley."

Gt. Central closes to passengers

After 87 years Brackley Railway Station has closed to passenger traffic. The end of line came at 12.04 a.m. on Sunday when the last train to leave the town was seen off by hundreds of railway enthusiasts who filled the train.

Also closed at the week-end was Woodford Halse Station, which follows the decision to close most of the former Great Central line between Marylebone, London and Sheffield via Aylesbury, Brackley, Rugby and Nottingham.

Extra buses will run on weekdays to replace the trains. These include services between Brackley and Aylesbury, Woodford Halse and Rugby and also an addition to the Banbury-Woodford Halse service which leaves from Banbury station at 9.16 p.m.

Rare bird
A bonus picture for any photographer's album, showing A4 60029 *Woodcock* at Nottingham 'Vic' on a 'down' Ian Allan special working which travelled from Paddington to Doncaster Works to Marylebone. The date was 24 April 1957 and the engine, in its immaculate state, is a real picture as it sits in platform 7 waiting for the right away.

Westerns at Weekday Cross
One of the finer workings of the Great Central London Extension section was the Bournemouth-Bradford express which provided a fair variety of stock. Here 'Hall' Class 6911 *Holker Hall* passes Weekday Cross signal cabin with a 'down' express to Bradford. The date is 1964, two years before the end of the line.

main lines. The famous train 'The Master Cutler' (which incidentally is still the fastest train between London and Sheffield) had been given over to working out of Kings Cross, and later St Pancras in 1957. The few trains were the York-Bristol, York-Poole, Manchester-Marylebone, plus a Sheffield-Swindon Mail and two Nottingham trains. And so on the last turn in the early hours of Sunday, 4 September 1966, the very last service of any kind through to London Marylebone steamed out from Nottingham. The last run used the Culworth-Banbury route with an engine change at Banbury. Banbury had been modernised and provided with a large area of sidings and a new interchange for the GC and LMS in 1959. The yard is now empty and the station underused,

proving what a 'white elephant' the reconstruction was.

The GC died with a strong spirit but feelings were mixed over its closure. For some, it gave the chance of track-lifting contracts; for some the chance of economy; for some, building a road-traffic haulage company; but to others, it was not just the closing of another government surplus railway. For many it was a career, a Lord and Master, an interest, but essentially the GC was always the last outpost of Main Line Steam. For one town, however, which ate, slept and drank railway, Woodford Halse & Hinton, the loss of the railway had the effect of creating a demoralised ghost town. At the closure 450 men were made redundant at Woodford. But worse still, the only factory there employed female

labour so skilled men found themselves sweeping floors, oiling machines and other unskilled tasks. They sought work as far afield as Chipping Warden, Daventry, Rugby and Leamington: some were lucky, however, and were transferred for diesel training on the Midland.

The old 'Vic' *Top*
'Stanier' Black Five 45208(25F) stands at Nottingham Victoria in platform 7 on a York–Bournemouth working. The year is 1949, when the then newly-formed British Railways were experimenting with locomotive and rolling stock liveries and one of the ideas which evolved was the writing of British Railways in bold letters on the tenders. Note the shiny panel on the locomotive boiler and the headboard

which has been reversed. This practice was usual because the engine would work southwards from Bradford to Leicester with another train before picking up the 'South Yorkshireman' and returning to its home depot.

All weep! Ave atque vale *Bottom*
The day is the 3 September 1966 and the place is Woodford Halse, already a mere

shadow of its former self. Sixty-seven years after the opening the mourners are present, to lament the line's passing as the final semi-fast farewell train hauled by 44484, complete with wreath, leaves for Marylebone with the 5.15pm ex Nottingham. In the early hours of the following morning, the very last train passed through Woodford in front of a handful of spectators, some of whom had been at the opening ceremony.

146

Gone Completely

Chapter Seven

GONE COMPLETELY

'GREAT CENTRAL RAILWAY – SHEFFIELD VICTORIA TO BANBURY'

Unmitigated England
  Came swinging down the line
That day the February sun
  Did crisp and crystal shine.
Dark red at Kirkby Bentinck stood
  A steeply gabled farm
'Mid ash trees and a sycamore
  In charismatic calm.
A village street – a manor house –
  A church – then, tally ho!
We pounded through a housing scheme
  With tellymasts a-row,
Where cars of parked executives
  Did regimented wait
Beside administrative blocks
  Within the factory gate.
She waved to us from Hucknall South
  As we hooted round a bend,
From a curtained front-room window did
  The diesel driver's friend.
Through cuttings deep to Nottingham
  Precariously we wound;
The swallowing tunnel made the train
  Seem London's Underground.

Above the fields of Leicestershire
  On arches we were borne
And the rumble of the railway drowned
  The thunder of the Quorn;
And silver shone the steeples out
  Above the barren boughs;
Colts in a paddock ran from us
  But not the solid cows;
And quite where Rugby Central is
  Does only Rugby know.
We watched the empty platform wait
  And sadly saw it go.
By now the sun of afternoon
  Showed ridge and furrow shadows
And shallow unfamiliar lakes
  Stood shivering in the meadows.
Is Woodford church or Hinton church
  The one I ought to see?
Or were they both too much restored
  In 1883?
I do not know. Towards the west
  A trail of glory runs
And we leave the old Great Central line
  For Banbury and buns.

The late Sir John Betjeman

These former Great Central territories which the late Sir John Betjeman so vividly recalls in his fine poem *GREAT CENTRAL, SHEFFIELD TO VICTORIA TO BANBURY*, were neither just a name on the map nor a place of business, they were actually part of the make-up of the line even though some of them had only the distinction of being small villages. It was because of this that the railway became trackless and totally devoid of life. In fact, the closure of a railway such as the GC always leaves a scar when it has been moved but however much one tries to destroy a line, a tell-tale vestige will always appear. The question of land used by a railway always poses a problem from the point of view of disposal and British Rail's general policy at closure was to hand over the land to County Councils to redistribute between farmers, planners and other purchasers. Some of the remarkable relics left mainly in the form of

Twixt Basford and Bulwell
From the brow of the hill this fine view of Bulwell can be seen, with the formation of the old railway junctions very much in evidence in the background. Bagthorpe Junction, its official title, was known to locals and railwaymen alike as the 'Rathole' because of the way the lines burrowed in and out of the hillside. The area left by the railway is now being used for a housing scheme by Nottingham City Council.

Previous Page
Class D11/1 'Director' 62668 *Jutland* sits under the wires at Sheffield Victoria on 10 August, 1960.

viaducts and tunnels have alas, fallen foul of the demolition man's ball and explosives, mostly to provide hardcore for roads.

At Annesley, where the line began, the initial effect of the train-shed closing meant redundancies but here, like Leicester, other forms of employment could be found as well as other uses for the site, since here was a large industrial area which could survive without any railways. South of Annesley much evidence remains of the railway at Hucknall and Bulwell Common where the viaduct still stands proudly. The course, being easy to define despite some of the subsequent industrial and residential developments, leads into a whole series of junctions known as Bagthorpe curves, though the locals knew this area as the 'Rathole' because of the way the lines burrowed into the cuttings. A quarter-of-a-mile south of Bagthorpe Junction lay New Basford station and yard which is used as a general park and coal yard. The stationmaster's house and entrance are still visible from Haydn Road, while in the yard itself the large goods shed dominates the scene. Basford was the beginning of the long cutting lead-ing up to the north end of Sherwood Rise tunnel which can be viewed but not walked, as both ends are blocked off. Carrington station lay between Sherwood Rise tunnel and Mansfield Road tunnel, which one can still walk as the northern end can be reached from the station whose platforms and footbridge walls are very much in evidence. At the end of the 'down' platform an old concrete signal post stands forlornly with its ravaged control box. Returning to the Mansfield Road tunnel, entering from the northern end, the first thing one notices is the construction. The hole is carved out of the sandstone with only the roof being covered in the usual engineers' blue brick which makes the tunnel look in-complete. Under the booking office, which is now a newsagents' and private residence, the tunnel has a short stretch from the north-ern portal which is surrounded with a complete brick face. A short distance into the tunnel by the side of the 'up' line there is a rather faded ¾ mile post which, fortu-nately, hunters have missed. Walk-ing through in the darkness, one can imagine 'The South Yorkshire-man' and the 'Runners' and 'Windcutters' roaring through the

New Basford   *Top left*
Christmas Eve 1984 and the author has managed to obtain a close-up of the fairly well preserved Goods Transfer shed which lay in the coal yard. The main line was to the left at the back of the building, while the station was at the Annesley end of the yard.

New Basford   *Top right*
Taken from Haydn Road, the station house stands rather forlornly as the yard keeper's cottage. The windows still have frames painted in the old Midland Region maroon. The actual entrance to the island platform was gained from a staircase leading up from the road, 100 yards further down on the left.

Manfield Road north end
Through the haze of the autumn sun it is just possible to make out the somewhat delapidated northern portal of Mansfield Road tunnel. The picture was taken from the site of the 'up' platform of Nottingham's Carrington station.

Nottingham 'Vic' 'All weep'
A rather sorry sight as preparations are made for the beginning of a new era in the form of the new shopping centre. The buildings have all been demolished and all the track has been removed save for the two lines leading into the tunnel which were retained for goods purposes. The turntable bed is on the left along with odd stacks of track lengths, ready for removal by road. Note the sad-looking buffer stop by the tunnel entrance.

tunnel. Sadly, that has all gone now but the atmosphere still remains. However, life in the city up above has been largely unaltered since the passing of the Great Central. Apart from the occasional rail keys and pieces of ballast, the tunnel has been strewn with abandoned wares from supermarkets and households. Other remains from the railway days survive such as electrical wire trunking and some of the cabling used for signalling, which lies burnt

on the ground near the southern portal. A hundred yards from the southern exit an old two-aspect colour-light signal still stands complete with ladder and even a light bulb in one of the casings. Near this signal are two ten-foot recesses, one on each side which were used for men at work and the storage of tools.

Leaving the tunnel, the southern end is now used to advertise a local building society, employing the trains theme. Access can still be

Razed to the ground
Looking towards Parliament Street and the tunnel through to Weekday Cross, all is gone apart from the two goods lines and the road down to the dock platform which still exists. Here again, there was another turntable, but the two in the complex often played havoc with the turning of engines due to their being too short to take large locos. Note the colours on the ground, the white being the platform areas while the dark grey is where the tracks stood.

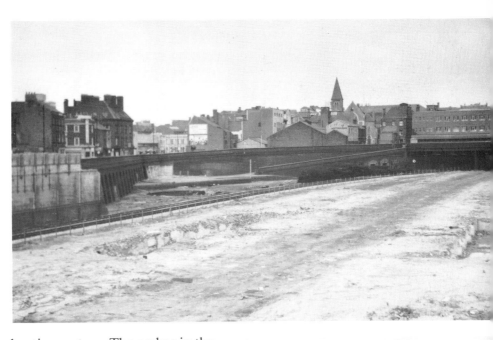

gained from the southern end to the tunnel as a door has been cleverly incorporated in the hoarding. One frosty morning five years ago, looking down from above at the tunnel and the small part of the area that was once Nottingham Victoria, I was able to trace out the pattern of the turntable and some of the other bits and pieces of buildings which made the site look like an archaeologist's dream. Nottingham itself is an interesting place which has become a modern pedestrianised city with a mixture of old and new buildings making it very much a go-ahead place: the most impressive feature of the city is the Town Hall with the typical northern nickname of the Council House. Nottingham City Council has made good use of the land vacated by the Great Central and Great Northern station by developing a shopping area there, known as the Victoria Centre. The complex consists of luxury flats, restaurants, department stores, small shops, the original hotel and clock tower, and bus station. At the bus station end one cannot help wondering why the railway was abandoned in favour of providing a local and long-distance bus/coach station.

Thurland Street tunnel lies buried beneath the city, at the southern end of the Victoria complex before reappearing at the site of Weekday Cross Junction. The tunnel now carries two large pipes in its deepest recesses to the shopping centre as these form part of a

heating system. The arches in the viaducts and the lattice structures still remain as a reminder, crossing the streets at all angles since many of them have now become workshops or the havens of small businesses. Moving down to Arkwright Street the scene changes quite dramatically as the station and any trace of the railway has been erased as far as Wilford Road bridge by a series of new council-built houses. From the bridge over the Trent at Wilford, as far as Ruddington, it is possible to trace the course more or less exactly. On the embankment, south of the River Trent, stands a tall signal post with gantry though it is now devoid of arms.

At Ruddington a short stretch of line remains as far as Loughborough, to cater for trains to and from the army ordnance depot sidings (now closed). This long siding is also used for gypsum workings from East Leake and Gotham gypsum mines. At the time of closure of the London Extension, access to this line was gained from Weekday Cross Junction via the old Grantham line but later, to simplify workings, this portion was lifted and a connection was installed south of the Loughborough Midland station. However, the future now looks bleak, for the line is inoperative beyond Rushcliffe Halt. At Ruddington the platforms still exist along with the rusting rails, weed-ridden sidings and the odd bare signal post. Returning to Rushcliffe, a double track still exists

Bird's eye view
High above the streets of Nottingham the view of Nottingham Victoria has somewhat changed. The old Victorian facade has disappeared and all that is left now is the clock tower and the Victoria hotel. To mark the conversion from station to shopping centre a plaque was unveiled on the side of the clock tower just inside the western entrance to the centre.

Wilford Road monument

The sun sets on Wilford Road railway viaduct on 1 November 1984. No longer do 'Runners' run or 'Windcutters' wind their way through the tunnels of Nottingham–Annesley. Here the remains of the line from the south come to an abrupt end as the land has been re-used around Arkwright Street for housing.

Barnston tunnel

The first tunnel after Nottingham on the route to London still carries the single track as far as Loughborough Chord Juction. The undergrowth has already begun to creep back. An idyllic spot between East Leake and Loughborough.

Rushciffe halt

Taken by a fellow enthusiast on the Ruddington Requiem Railtour. The scene has changed quite dramatically since operational days. The 'up' main has become a mere siding and long shunt into the gypsum works sidings. The platforms are still just visible under the bridge and the station is noted for being one of the three non-island layouts on the London Extension. Its proximity to the roadbridge avoided the need for a footbridge.

through the station which, along with Nottingham's Carrington and Arkwright Street stations, are the only non-island platforms on the London Extension. Here, too, a number of sidings along with the well-preserved station platforms provide suitable interest. Similar remains can be seen at East Leake which was the last stop before Loughborough Central. Eventually it is possible that the line to Ruddington will fall into the hands of the Main Line Steam Trust. The latter, better known as the Great Central Railway Company 1976, is succeeding in preserving one of the most scenically beautiful sections of the route to Rothley via Quorn and Woodhouse which passses through the Charnwood forest and over the Swithland reservoir. The group was set up in 1969 as the Main Line Preservation Group but it was not until two years later that progress was made. However, the company suffered many setbacks, before finally beginning services in 1976 (although a supervised BR steam service had begun two years earlier). The Great Central company runs a single track and is hoping to restore the section to Belgrave and Birstall as well as installing a loop at Quorn station. The extension to Birstall will bring the line down to the outskirts of Leicester. The Great Central also boasts a large section of locomotives and coaches and has added attractions of Schools Steamings and is particularly noted for its 'on train' catering on the 'Charnwood Forester'.

At Leicester, along Abbey Lane, sections of the viaducts can be seen but much of the structure has disappeared in the centre of town. The station area now houses an industrial estate with small units and a car park. Upon closer inspection, it is possible to find the odd traces of the old station platforms. The railway has also left behind it a trail of ballast and one or two buildings from the glorious Great Central days. The reception area and booking hall, also the parcels office, remain and are used now for industrial purposes. Above one of the gates, evidence of the past can be seen from the lintel which proudly exclaims 'Great Central

Railway Parcels Offices'. The other remains are those of the brick arches and large girder bridges that go to make up the area known as Leicester West Bridge. Further down the line one can still trace the route through Whetstone and Ashby Magna stations which are now just open spaces lying parallel to the M1 motorway. Similarly,

Weekday Cross
Trackbed and viaducts still remain on both lines for a short distance as a monument to the existence of a railway. Taken from Middle Hill (formerly Drury Hill) escape lane, the line off to the left was the spur for Grantham while the one going straight ahead was that to London. The steam is not from the ghost 'Master Cutler' but from the central heating system of the Victoria Centre which has a steam vent in the bottom left-hand corner of the picture.

Loughborough Central
Shortly after the revival of the station, the scene looks fairly impressive. The goods shed is now isolated from the line as it belongs to a local haulier. Also to the right-hand side of the picture, good use has been put to many old covered van and container bodies. The locomotive on the old 'down' main line is ex Norwegian State Railways Class 21c 2-6-0 No. 377 which hauled the first train on the MLST in June 1973, while the two little engines are 'Robert Nelson' No. 4, a Hunslet built in 1936 and D4279 'Arthur Wright' built by John Fowler, working empty stock into platform 1.

Lutterworth is desolate and devoid of life.

Rugby, the next port of call along the route to London and just before the run up to the Great Central station from the north end, lay one of the magnificent viaducts. Sadly, the brick arches have now been demolished but part of the 'Birdcage' girder bridge remains looking down upon the wires of the West Coast main line. It was at this long viaduct that the southern division for the building contracts had begun. More indeed remains of this stretch, even though it closed three years before the line north of Rugby Central. Today the lead up to the platform at Hillmorton Road can be defined clearly though little remains of the cattle dock and goods yard as these have been acquired for use as a timber yard. In the cutting in which the station lies, one can see the platform and the lines formation as it veers off towards Braunston & Willoughby, which is the next station on the route. The latter is barely traceable, if not impossible to see. At Staverton a gaping hole has been left by the demolition of what was an impressive structure amidst the beautiful scenery of the Northamptonshire uplands. From here as far as Catesby, all the bridges remain including the viaduct and the stone bridge which leads up to the approach of the Catesby tunnel. On top of the northern portal of Catesby tunnel sits the everimposing residence of the gunpowder plotter Robert Catesby, noted for his part in the attempt to blow up the Houses of Parliament in 1603.

The Catesby tunnel can be defined by mounds and breather shafts which appear at various points along the roads in the vicinity. South of Catesby, which is still walkable with the aid of a good pair of wellingtons and a torch, is Charwelton, once an important exchange point for a local quarry which extracted ironstone.

Here in the middle of nowhere is the remains of a station and stationmaster's house which is now

Swithland reservoir
Reflections! The arch of one of the viaducts appears like a complete circle in the shimmering water of the reservoir. A truly beautiful spot enhanced by the passage of the occasional steam train. The reservoir still supplies most of Leicester's water.

Rothley 'Runner'
After negotiating the small island platform at Rothley, loco J39 heads over the points towards the permanent way compound with an engineers' train. The loco, purchased by a local enthusiast and fitted with side tanks, has now left the Great Central owing to its unsuitability for hauling passenger trains.

a private dwelling and this section of land, once popular with walkers, has just recently become private property and is used as a shoot. From Charwelton to Woodford the land was more or less dominated by railway lines since Woodford played a vital role in the operation of the Great Central with its expansive marshalling yards, junctions, locomotive depot and passenger station. The wartime yards are now fields, although odd buildings and the coarse nature of the ground show that once something interesting happened there. The sheds were demolished by the marines after many unsuccessful attempts had been made to attract Rover

Cars or York Trailers to set up a factory there. Indeed, it required four lots of explosive to raze the building to the ground. Watkin would have been pleased!

My first visit to Woodford was a memorable one as there was a splendid sunset over the Catesby end of the town. At that time Woodford's station platforms and station house were both still in evidence but since then a local fairground company had the platforms removed in order to park their vehicles. The station yard is now Forestry Commission land and has been made a walking area. On the Byfield Road a new road called Great Central Way leads into a

Leicester Central
Great Central Street where the station proudly stood. When this picture was taken a service was still running between Rugby and Nottingham. With track lifting in the station area, spare space became available for car parking, hence the large board on the roadway wall. One of the platform roofs can be seen although now these have been demolished and a 1980s style industrial area occupies the site.

Leicester's epitaph
An ornate lintel proclaiming 'Great Central Parcels Offices' proudly stands as a memorial to the once great line. Note the little bushes appearing out of the capping bricks.

West bridge
Looking through the skew girder bridge towards the station along the trackbed, the line is now no more than a desolate path snaking its way through the city.

small industrial estate carved out of part of the yards. This was created under the Northampton County Council revitalisation plan for Woodford. South of the station area it is possible to trace the three chords of the junction. One of these latter parts has been in use as a tip. About half-a-mile from Woodford, the Culworth-Banbury link can be found, along with the site of the station slightly further along in the Helmdon direction, which is now part of a farm. From Culworth to Brackley the only two features which are predominant, apart from the road bridges, are the viaduct at Helmdon which served two purposes: one was to pass over the river and the other to bridge the Northampton & Banbury Junction Railway. Helmdon station yard, like many others, is in use as a coal yard. The other major relic of engineering feats on the GC in this area is the large cutting near the little village of Sulgrave, home of the Washington family.

Brackley has suffered little change and although the station buildings still exist, the land is up for sale and the garage and new car storage depot have folded up. Unfortunately the viaduct was demolished for hardcore for

improving the A43 road. Another item which survives is the massive water tower which is in use as a large tank for a local farm. From here down to Finmere there are no special uses and the track bed lies derelict except for a stretch which carries power lines. In the station area the platforms remain, as at Calvert.

At Calvert the rails begin, and up until 1977 the yards were used for the transfer of brick trains from the London Brickworks but most of this traffic now goes by road. Its present use is to receive refuse trains from the GLC which release waste into the brick pits. Due to the volume of traffic a massive container crane has been constructed here. Other areas which were GC, like Ashenden-Akeman Street, have been removed. Akeman Street is used by UK Fertilizers and the Grendon MoD establishment and has one long siding which branches off the Calvert line. Wotton station is now a tastefully converted single-storey residence and one would hardly know that it had been a station. On the section between Ashendon and Princes Risborough little has changed except for a drastic track rationalisation and the singling of the line between Princes Risborough and Kings Sutton in 1968. The stations at Haddenham and Ilmer have long since been removed, along with West Wycombe. West Wycombe yards are now used as a BRS truck rental depot.

Since Marylebone retains a lot of its character and has a very slim service, except during morning and evening peak hours, it has a rather interesting spin-off for BR in off-peak hours: it is often let out to film companies who use the station especially when historic scenes are required. The station has often featured in cinema and TV films. Of course this is not the only change that Marylebone station complex has seen since the 1960s. At the time of opening, the coal and goods depots built to the north of the station occupied thirty-seven acres. Much of this development replaced housing and coincidentally, when these depots were closed, the land was acquired by the GLC and developed once again for housing.

The whole line, even though nearly erased, still captures one's deepest enthusiasm and just by walking short sections of the track-bed in and around Nottingham, Catesby, Leicester and Woodford and searching out some of the stations, it is possible to imagine how the GC must have been 'The Line for Gentlemen'. However the whole company, although they put on better facilities than other main lines and ran an efficient enterprise, never really made a substantial profit. Perhaps the Watkin empire

was too ambitious or the line might never have been intended to tear through the beautiful countryside in central England. The whole venture might have worked if Watkin had bought running rights on the Midland and then run his channel tunnel. We know that Watkin took the wrong choice but, alas, being the last main railway he had to take the central England route.

This was a major setback before he even started but, had a little more planning been used and less stations been created miles from the villages they were supposed to serve, the problem could have been rectified and the GC might still have been running today.

Just a bridge
The sad remains of the first station on the Northern Division of the old Great Central London Extension, Lutterworth is now devoid of the trains. Unlike Ashby Magna, access to the station platform was gained from the road below by a staircase built into the bridge in the picture. The main part of the platform lay the photographer's side of the bridge, but one of the buildings was isolated on a short stretch of platform the 'gasometer' side. Note the trees to the right of the picture, which were planted by the Great Central.

Ashby Magna
Road versus rail. The railway followed the M1 motorway between Shawell and Whetstone and the picture shows a youthful motorway in the background, taken from the local station at Ashby Magna, as the writing on the platform edging stone shows. The date is 1969, the year of closure. The site of the old goods yard has been buried under the motorway embankment and only the weigh house remains.

After closure
Dunton Bassett tunnel in the early 1970s after track lifting. The tunnel was only very short in length and emerged at Ashby Magna station, which can be seen framed in the northern portal. The access bridge to the platform shows clearly where the staircase led down to the platform from the road above.

The bird has flown   *Opposite top*
North of Rugby Central two portions of what was nicknamed the 'Birdcage' bridge still stand as a reminder of the old London Extension and have probably never been removed because of disrupting the busy electrified West Coast Main Line. No longer do GC trains fly through the Avon valley on this superb viaduct.

Rugby Central   *Opposite bottom*
Only the platforms and trackbed remain. This photograph, looking north, shows the formation of the 'up' line and the way the line curved away in the cutting. The brick-filled gap was where the unusually large ticket office stood and the upright between the two bridges shows the remains of the stairway to the trains.

Perhaps a slight variation in its course might have attracted more business. Despite the inhibitions the author believes that the GC was purely a freight route and if this aspect of the market had been expanded, with modern rolling stock and the establishment of road/rail container depots, it might have kept a fair share of traffic on the rails. The ideal layout would have been to provide such centres at strategic points like Calvert, Brackley, Woodford & Hinton, Rugby, Leicester and Nottingham. South of Aylesbury the passenger services had always been quite passable and it would have been essential to retain this as a commuter line. If a plan of this nature had been implemented a fast efficient freight route to the north and the south would have been provided. Calvert is on the junction with the Bletchley-Oxford line; Brackley is on the A43 trunk road from Oxford to Northampton. Round Woodford, as can be seen today, the line once catered for the exchange and sorting of trucks due to the massive expanse of derelict marshalling yards. If this had been modernised Woodford could have become the centre of operations for trains to Sheffield, London, Banbury and South Wales.

Rugby, Leicester and Nottingham already had long-established stations and the advent of the GC posed no real serious threat to the rival Midland. These duplicates should never have been built but, instead, freight depots to serve local areas by road from railheads. Nevertheless the railway provided employment for many people and the tremendous effect it had in the larger areas can be seen at the time of closure.

A number of questions have to be considered today about the line and the form of transport which has taken over from the railway. It seems ironical that road transport made such a comeback in an era when Britain was busy attempting to reshape and modernise railways. The building of Britain's first motorway, the M1, was designed to improve communications and bypass bottlenecks to create a traffic flow unimpeded by poor routes. Since its construction, the M1 has suffered from the effects of ever-increasing capacities of lorries and buses unsuitable for such a road.

Many people have argued, and quite rightly so, that it is more costly to transport goods by road and, apart from the cost, the question of conservation and a pollution-free countryside are matters for consideration. For instance, heavy lorries are damaging small villages and the volume of traffic on some smaller road are causing the road to subside and so fracture underground pipes. On the motorways the density of vehicles has caused

the road surfaces to crack up in some places. The repair bill will be massive.

One cannot help thinking that the retention of a fully operative rail network would not only have provided a suitable means of transport but a faster and more economical method of delivering goods to firms and passengers. The motorways cost in the region of £1,500,000 to build and if this money had been used on improving Britain's railways and reducing the losses made by BR, the amount of traffic on Britain's roads (especially long distance) would have been halved. A train is capable of taking the equivalent of thirty lorry loads using a very small amount of fuel. In the long term the opportunity to save hydrocarbon fuels, which are becoming precious, is all too apparent. By far the best system would have been to link trunk route stations to a series of main roads which can be more economically maintained than their big brothers, the motorways.

The M1 motorway is very costly to maintain and a poor substitute for a line such as the GC might have been, had its route been somewhat different. The GC, by contrast, although disused for nearly

twenty years, still has traces of some of the magnificent bridges and tunnels which remain in pretty good order, while the motorway is crumbling.

A question always raised is, did the closure of the GC really improve the financial position or was it just a means to an end to fill the motorway with traffic? The result of Government policy has been that in most places communications have reverted to what they were before 1899. The cutting-off of the GC, in the long run, was shortsighted because the Governments of recent years have been no better off and have failed to make railways into a profitable venture. The decaying motorways bypass towns and do not attract industry, but an efficient railway does.

Lord Beeching should have advertised the railways and made an all-out effort to capture business and attract commercial enterprises to the main GC towns like Woodford and Brackley and others. Also the marketing of private owner wagons would have been a suitable way of earning a greater revenue. Most people realise that it costs twice as much to demolish a railway and pay off its workers and then embark on a

Woodford Halse: only memories
Devoid of life and trackless. This was the scene on the last day of operations on the section between Aylesbury and Rugby Central. The buildings were still standing when this shot was taken. The small addition tacked onto the right-hand side of the main shed was provided in connection with the coming of the diesels. It never saw much service as Woodford was graced with only four shunters in the end. The removal of the depot made Woodford a ghost village.

project like a motorway. It would not be so bad if motorway construction was of the same quality as railways have been.

Perhaps a different route might have attracted more custom: *i.e.* taking the route of the Metropolitan line from Quainton to Verney Junction, and then to Buckingham and Brackley, following the actual route to Woodford, and passing Daventry on to Rugby and Leicester, where it would join the Midland from St Pancras to Nottingham and Sheffield.

However, from the evidence provided one reaches the inevitable conclusion that the GC was a railway which appeared too late as part of an already established network. In spite of this, all who worked on it made desperate attempts throughout its history to make it into a profitable venture. It survived until long-distance road traffic became a threat with with advent of motorways in the 1960s. The age of coal was passing gradually with its replacement by oil due to the expansion and new technology in this field. The railways had to change their form of power from steam to diesel, and subsequently electric traction, in an all-out effort to enhance the quality

of the service they could provide.

The GC, however, remained steam-based until the end in 1966 and 1969, as it was not to be included in the modernisation of British Rail. Instead the M1 motorway was constructed at exorbitant cost to convey traffic which the GC would previously have transported.

The rundown was definitely a mistake in the eyes of many people who believe that investment in the railways freight traffic would have served the line. The GC, although closed, has not lost its identity completely since its trackbed and bridges still stand as a monument to those who built it, worked on it and managed the companies who controlled it.

Those who were fortunate enough to work on the GC devoted their lives in service to it, in fulfilment of part, at least, of Sir Edward Watkin's dream. Although of his railway empire all that remains is a preserved stretch of track from Belgrave to Loughborough (operated by the MLS Trust) and in the south, the very flourishing Railway Society at Quainton Road, yet the unquenchable spirit of the GC has survived into the new 'Age of the Train'.

Middle of nowhere
Wild life and foliage really have taken their toll in this picture taken twenty years after the closure of the station. Helmdon was a typical example of the island principle platforms and set in the middle of the barren Northamptonshire countryside. Helmdon has not really been affected by the coming or going of the railway.

Station Road
Little has changed since the fateful day in 1966. Woodford's colony still stands as a reminder to its more prosperous days, as does the railway bridge at the bottom of the hill. For the residents, railways are still very much a talking point, especially at the Woodford Halse & Hinton Social Club.

The viaduct
Standing out amidst the beautiful farmlands of Northamptonshire is Helmdon's nine-arch viaduct which stands to the north of the station. It is still possible to walk across the viaduct and as one does the formation of the old Northampton & Banbury Railway can be seen, which also had a station at Helmdon.

Brackley Central
Whilst the actual platforms have long since disappeared, the main station building still stands. The entrance to the footbridge can be seen above the arch, though now of course it is bricked up. Because of the worry that the station would cause hold-ups on the main road, the station building was built in a layby parallel to the platforms. The trees were planted when the line was built, to help camouflage the railway and the station buildings.

Brackley Central
Catering for modern needs, a well-preserved station building now acts as a tyre and exhaust centre. Brackley station ceased to operate as a passenger carrying station on 3 September 1966.

Along the line
The formation can clearly be seen from the line of trees and here a new use has been found, namely carrying pylons and power lines. the site is between Brackley and Finmere.

Near Finmere
Even farm tracks were provided with elaborate crossings as the Great Central, with its policy of speed and efficiency, had no type of crossings on the London Extension. This skew girder bridge shows the extensive lengths the contractors went to.

Calvert station
Weedridden but still in use, Calvert provides a fine example of what the railway was, and is, like. Closed in 1963 to passengers, the station still sees many freight workings and the odd special train passing through. The line skirting the platform on the left was the former 'down' main, whilst the 'up' main is still kept in good running order to cater for the GLC landfill trains which use the sidings, where there are transfer facilities for the containers.

Calvert station
Looking towards Aylesbury, the 'up' line is still in good condition and the curve off to the 'up' yard can be determined by the line of the broken light poles. The 'down' line has been re-arranged to accommodate Calvert's most recent acquisition, the freightliner crane which deals with trains like the one seen further down the siding.

Preservation
A prominent nameboard displays the name Quainton Road in somewhat disproportionate letters. Quainton is now the home of England's largest collection of industrial locomotives.

Quainton Road
Taken one fine sunny Saturday afternoon, the picture is almost timeless when one looks at the station's condition and the GWR 'Pannier' tank which is steaming towards platform 3 with the vintage train. The 'down' track through platform 2 was lifted when the line closed in 1966. The 'up' line is still used for freight and on bank holidays the line is used by the 'Quaintonian' which plies to and from the centre from Aylesbury.

St Trinian's or Marylebone?
The bus indicator and the uniforms show something special is happening; the making of a film at Londons 'Most Suitable' terminus, namely Marylebone. Where would the film crews go if this beautiful relic of the Golden Age of Railways disappears? The building over the road is the old Great Central Hotel, now the headquarters of British Rail.

Opposite page
Under the vast roof at Marylebone station a 4-car DMU waits to depart from platform 2 with the 11.10am working to Aylesbury.

Where the Rails Begin

Calvert North
It is hard to imagine that this rather remote and overgrown area of Bucks was once part of the Great Central main line. The line, now lifted, went due north to Nottingham. Where the tree silhouettes itself against the sky was a bridge crossing the London North Western, Oxford–Bletchley line. The hut on the right of the picture heralded the junction for the short spur to the latter line which was installed in 1940. Only the line on the right makes a physical connection today, used for freight, stock movements and special workings, while the one on the left is now just a siding for landfill trains – a far cry from its heyday.

Chapter Eight

WHERE THE RAILS BEGIN

With the closure of the GC as a through route, the main route through High Wycombe lost half its custom and subsequently, with the advent of diesel unit service, the trains have become less regular with a train every two hours to Banbury. In late 1976 the line between Princes Risborough and Banbury was singled up as far as Aynho Junction. Today there are only two trains through to Birmingham which is a far cry from the 1950s and 1960s. A few goods trains still use the Wycombe line, carrying oil to Thame or cement to Chinnor or waste to Calvert via the former Princes Risborough-Aylesbury link (still used for peak services). In 1971 the Wycombe GW&GC line began again to be used for steam trials when preservation specials and enthusiast specials began to run over British Railway metals again.

Recently the Wycombe line has been a subject for discussion with regard to using Marylebone to its best ability and attracting passengers to travel on a projected long-haul steam route. While SLOA and BR were negotiating, a tragic accident occurred in December 1981 killing two schoolboys, a student and the driver. The accident occurred at Seer Green in the 75-foot cutting in adverse weather conditions when the 7.31am Banbury tain, packed with commuters, ploughed into the back of an empty train bound for Princes Risborough which had been stopped by a tree laden with snow.

Perhaps the latter is a sign that it is dangerous to allow railways to run down and that there is a necessity to remove antiquated signalling equipment which remains on certain lines. This particular factor is one which may be preventing an increased service, whether by steam or diesel, since modernising a secondary route would not be economically viable. Indeed, the line is coming under threat of closure yet again, mainly for this reason.

Alas, the GC is again labelled with the title 'duplicate main line' and there are moves afoot to bring about closure of its fine terminus at

Calvert North
Since the demolition of the signal box at Calvert and the drastic reduction of trackwork, operations have become controlled by two small ground frames, one of which is shown in the picture. The north frame controls access to the long siding that leads into the landfill depot from the north of the station.

Marylebone and the line as far as Northolt, which would remove the last vestiges of the Great Central London Extension from the map. The decision to close can be put down to a number of factors like service reduction and altering trends in government-subsidised transport systems and the desire by British Rail to recover the profits from the sale of the whole site.

It seems that as a result of the Serpell inquiry, local and commuter lines are once more likely to be subject to the threat of closure, repeating the scenario of the 1960s when the Beeching axe was wielded with great abandon over the GC lines. The Chiltern area will suffer not insignificantly if Marylebone is closed and the Buckinghamshire commuter operation re-distributed between Paddington and Baker Street. One immediate result, fore-shadowed by the recent rail strike, would be a tremendous upsurge in road traffic in the same fashion as when the London Extension closed. Coaches and cars are causing a considerable further loss of revenue to the railways and this situation might well provide valid justifica-

tion for further rail closures on economic grounds.

The use of Paddington as the terminus of the Aylesbury-London and Banbury-Wycombe-London routes, to which British Rail and others seem indissolubly wedded, is beset by two major difficulties, both obvious even to a casual observer: (1) density of main-line traffic already using this facility would inevitably upset the status and running of all trains because of their timetables being subject to disruption or being affected by any

Quainton Met Junction
Just north of the new station site at this point was the boundary between the Great Central and Metropolitan. Where the line curves the Metropolitan had a signal box which controlled the junction by the bridge to Verney Junction, whose formation follows the line of trees. The wide area either side of the single track in the foreground once contained the original station at Quainton until it became an important junction.

Quainton Station

Preparing for steam one hot summer day in 1984, the station is coming to life once more for the regular onslaught of train enthusiasts wanting to capture some of the atmosphere of the depot and the steam age alike. In the background the extensive exchange yards, once busy with goods trains, now provide ample accommodation for the preservation movement and its old vehicles, while the station itself sees a fair amount of patronage. On the far right of the picture is platform 3, once used by trains to Brill on the old Wotton Tramway, now used by the vintage train run of the Quainton Railway Society. Platform 2 on the old 'down' main served local trains though now it is trackless. The 'up' main still enjoys some use, while platform 1, which it serves occasionally, plays host to special stopping trains like the 'Quaintonian' and the 'Milton Keynes Shopper'.

Aylesbury Town

A damp summer Saturday morning sees Aylesbury a hive of activity. On the far right two DMUs are stabled in the small yard, while in platform 1 the 10.40am train to Marylebone awaits the right away. In the background are the main station buildings and the footbridge to platforms 3 and 4. The train from which the picture was taken, on the left, is the 9.15am Fakenham and Dereham Railtour which has just come off the Princes Risborough Branch.

number of exigencies like the withdrawal of Sunday working, as happened in the final years of the GC; (2) its less convenient location in respect of onward journeys for the city commuter whose interests we are considering rather more than those of the holidaymaker or less frequent traveller to the west country whose interests would be well served by the link with Paddington. It is not so long ago that British Rail tried running a commuter service into Paddington from the Wycombe-Banbury route but it ended up being withdrawn as it was yet another duplicate service which had failed. Therefore it goes to show that Paddington is not an ideal system.

When considering how one could reroute the services, there is little reason to try running trains via Old Oak Common West or the Greenford Loop, as these would consume too much time. Added to this the Wycombe-Maidenhead link is no longer a viable proposition as the land has now been converted into industrial units and handed over to private ownership, nor is there a link between High Wycombe and Bourne End.

Turning to the Aylesbury line, people are talking of electrifying the line to Aylesbury and providing a through run to Baker Street. However, this scheme is also beset by two major problems. The first is where and how could London Transport afford to electrify now, when it said it could not afford to in 1961, and this would mean that the line would be given as little trackwork and equipment as absolutely necessary. The second disadvantage of using the Baker Street line is the fact that the survival of minority lines, such as the Watford line, would be jeopardised with the introduction of extra services which Baker Street is not designed to cope with. Also one must not forget that in the days of the MET & GC joint line the stock used was far more suitable for commuter trains running over a longer distance.

When one considers these aspects it is quite easy to see how Marylebone came to be built and indeed the GW and GC joint line which was provided to bypass the Metropolitan bottleneck and relieve the pressure on the GWR Birmingham route. After all, Watkin built the GC specifically as a 'modern' line which would be able to help relieve the burden of traffic on other lines. Even though

Aylesbury South Junction
At this point the line from Princes Risborough joins the line from Amersham, seen in the foreground of the picture. The sidings where the DMUs are stabled once were busy with goods traffic. This picture was taken from the Princes Risborough branch. Note the fine array of semaphore signals controlled by Aylesbury south cabin.

FURY ERUPTS AS BR CLOSES MARYLEBONE

by Ian Paterson

NOW British Rail has announced it means to close Marylebone Station, resistance against the controversial move is growing.

Angry rail commuters in Chiltern District dread what they see as the disastrous consequences if the plan goes ahead — delays, inconvenience and generally a poorer service.

Passengers now using the local line to get to Marylebone will have to switch to what many regard as the far less satisfactory London Transport Baker Street Station.

And Gordon Dixon, chairman of the Federation of Metropolitan Line Users Committee, fears that the Chesham shuttle line could be axed as its limited number of passengers change to road transport.

Furious

The pressure group leader, who has been in the front line of protesters fighting to save Marylebone from extinction, said this week he was furious about BR's closure decision.

But, he said, he hoped enough pressure could be exerted at all levels to get the decision reversed. He said there was still time as BR has said closure was unlikely to take place for at least two years.

He said although it had been known for a long time that Marylebone was under threat, now that there was a very great possibility of it actually happening, opposition to it was strengthening.

Chesham and Amersham MP Sir Ian Gilmour and commuter groups in Buckinghamshire are incensed by the plan to shut down what they regard as an important amenity.

Now they are redoubling their efforts to preserve the station.

It was last week that the British Railways Board formally announced its intention to scrap Marylebone Station.

Savings

Letters explaining the position were sent to Buckinghamshire and Hertfordshire County Councils, four London boroughs, the City of Westminster Council, the GLC, the Transport Users Consultative Committees for London and the South-east and to the Central Transport Consultative Committee.

The letters said: "A preliminary study, undertaken jointly with London Transport, indicates that the closure of Marylebone Station and the approach lines from Harrow and Northolt would offer considerable savings by eliminating the wasteful duplication of services that now exists, while continuing to offer a service to the majority of existing passengers.

"Accordingly, the Board has decided to initiate the closure process, taking into account wherever possible the views of passengers and local authorities in formulating detailed proposals."

Formal closure proposals will be published under Section 56 of the 1962 Transport Act later this year.

British Rail says that if objections are received they will be considered by the Transport Users Consultative Committee and a final decision will be taken by the Secretary of State for Transport.

But BR added that even if agreement to close Marylebone was forthcoming closure was unlikely to take place for at least two years.

BR was opposed to the scheme to convert Marylebone Station into a coach station, turning railway track into roadway.

The Board had considered a report drawn up by consultants Coopers and Lyebrand Associates which had looked at the possibility of converting 10 lines into London into roads.

Only the Marylebone-Northolt route, said the report, presented a prima facie case for further study.

But the road on this stretch would be only 6.7 metres wide as against the standard 7.3 metres, with one narrower section only 5.9 metres wide.

It would have to be limited to cars only or, as an alternative, be designed for single-deck buses only, with some sections limited to single direction operation.

---

the railways do not carry as much traffic today, it seems silly to try to pack in extra services in other already over-used termini. The GC commuter network has always had a reputation for reliability and comfort and it still does today even though only the Southern commuter system remains.

Let us consider the advantages which Marylebone has, which would justify keeping it open. Following recent events at Paddington and on the Euston line it could well prove itself useful as a relief and overspill terminus for the latter two, a role it fulfilled admirably during the work on the electrification of the Euston-Glasgow line in 1963-6. Marylebone could receive and send out trains to and from Birmingham and receive diverted trains from Manchester via Bletchley, Calvert, Aylesbury and High Wycombe. Indeed, if there was demand, there might be good grounds for electrifying the GC out of Marylebone thus allowing cheaper running commuter services using modern class 317 EMU stock. This kind of service would also help to generate business in the Aylesbury, Princes Risborough and Wycombe areas as the line is becoming too little used.

If this option is not feasible, perhaps the more realistic and economically viable one in the future would entail the closure of Marylebone as has been put forward twice before. But if British Rail is to embark on such a scheme then they should consider the rerouting of trains into St Pancras, as was done with 'The Master Cutler' in 1957-8, when the demise of the GC was commencing.

Such rationalisation would entail a small number of modifications to the existing system which might, in part at least, be financed by the sale of the Marylebone site and adjacent properties belonging to BR. Of course, the Marylebone-Northolt line would make an ideal link to the line to Birmingham and Stratford-upon-Avon which could be used for steam-hauled specials thus encouraging tourist potential. Under this plan Marylebone, because of its size, would make an excellent stabling point and museum for steam engines and

---

County council adds more power to the protesters' campaign

Rail battle hots up

BUCKS County Council has joined the campaign to stop the threatened closure of Marylebone Station.

And it will have the backing of South Bucks District Council for its plans to organise a formal protest to the watchdog body, the Transport Users' Consultative Committee.

In its submissions to the TUCC, which will make a recommendation on the station's future to the Secretary of State for Transport, Nicholas Ridley, the council will say that the British Rail proposals ignore the wishes and convenience of passengers.

Chairman of the county council's public transport sub-committee, Mr Kenneth Ross, said the direct service from Aylesbury to Paddington via High Wycombe would take up to 30 minutes longer than existing Aylesbury to Marylebone trains.

"And to put more Underground trains into an already busy Baker Street station would adversely affect peak hour reliability," said Mr Ross.

The decision of the district council to oppose the closure plans came at a meeting of its amenities committee.

Meanwhile the people who would be directly affected by the closure have been out in force to make their feelings known.

Travellers joined a special shopping train from

By Jerry Charge

Marylebone to Milton Keynes on Saturday to protest at the station's threatened closure and also to push for an extension of the Marylebone line to the fast growing town.

The diesel train was chartered by the Aylesbury and District Railway Association.

Among those on the train was Greater London Council chairman Illtyd Harrington.

A GLC spokesman said: "Mr Harrington was supporting the protesters against the station's closure. It cuts across all GLC policy of improving services rather than cutting back."

● The assistant area manager of British Rail was bombarded with questions about Marylebone Station at a meeting of Seer Green and Jordans Society.

But Mike Carroll said he had come to speak about the future of railways and dodged questions about how the disabled would manage when Marylebone closes.

● Illtyd Harrington outside Gerrards Cross station supporting the campaign against the closure of Marylebone.

Princes Risborough
Two signal boxes existed at Risborough, one south of the station which controlled the goods yard, and one at the north, pictured here. This box contained a 100-lever frame the length of a cricket pitch, which controlled this really busy station that served what was no more than a small market town. Note the stationary tankers which have just come off the Thame Branch which diverges behind the box.

carriages, while the station could be converted into a leisure complex leaving two platforms free for the excursion traffic. This would seem to be the most logical idea as very little work or disruption would be caused and everybody would be happy.

Recently Marylebone has been the subject of a £50,000 survey which was commissioned in light of the finds of the Serpell Report on converting railways into roads. The cost of conversion for Marylebone to Northolt was estimated at £21 million and eventually the proposal for an express busway out of Marylebone was dropped on the grounds of safety and expense. The main argument was over the tunnels under Lords and the ques-

tion of profit which might have been recouped.

However, it is clear that BR will probably opt for the most economic solution in the end and the one that is best for its passengers, namely St Pancras. The advantages are obvious on the administrative side, namely that both Wycombe-Banbury and Aylesbury routes would remain under the aegis of the Midland and, secondly, the timetable would need little altering to accommodate the extra traffic. The joining of the lines would provide scope for all kinds of possibilities in the manner of the Bedford Midland connection. Indeed there is no physical connection between the two lines at present but there are two sites where a link could be incorporated at a small cost, namely Neasden (*Fig. 1*) and West Hampstead (*Fig. 2*).

The line could either diverge at Neasden, in which case two new chords would have to be installed which would connect both lines to the Brent Junction-Cricklewood section, whence it would join the Midland main to St Pancras – well served by main line and underground alike – for onward journeys; or it could connect at West Hampstead, but this would not have as many advantages. Apart from the saving of time for the City commuter, Brent Junction line also provides an ideal link with the Southern Region. At present the connection is used for freight-working carrying oil, stone, coal, refuse and fertilisers to the northernmost points on the line.

The opening of the line to Cricklewood for passengers would allow extra savings as the ageing stocks of DMUs could be replaced by rakes of upgraded MK1 carriage stock for commuter work. These

could be stabled at Cricklewood depot thus reducing maintenance costs and improving the standards of comfort and service offered by a line that has been renowned for its superior travel since the beginning of the GC.

However, among the many factors which determine the economic running of commuter services, three in particular need serious consideration in any proposed restructuring of the last remaining part of the GC network, namely (1) flexibility of services, which the change in operation would provide; (2) the concentration of passengers from outlying districts by means of local bus services whose timetables are interlinked with trains; and (3) an improved fares structure to attract the maximum number of regular passengers (the constant increase in fares is counterproductive and not the way to approach the problem).

The Chiltern railway network is undoubtedly a very important asset. Any wholesale transfer of rail passengers or freight to road

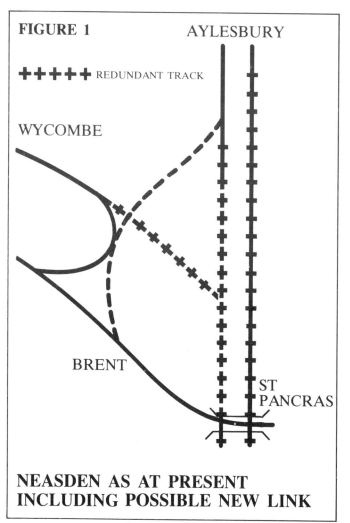

FIGURE 1

AYLESBURY

+ + + + + REDUNDANT TRACK

WYCOMBE

BRENT

ST PANCRAS

NEASDEN AS AT PRESENT INCLUDING POSSIBLE NEW LINK

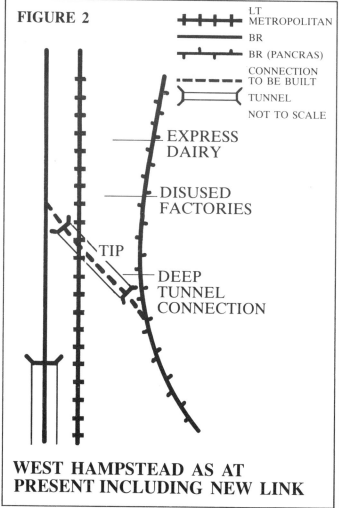

FIGURE 2

+ + + + LT METROPOLITAN

— BR

— BR (PANCRAS)

– – – CONNECTION TO BE BUILT

TUNNEL

NOT TO SCALE

EXPRESS DAIRY

DISUSED FACTORIES

TIP

DEEP TUNNEL CONNECTION

WEST HAMPSTEAD AS AT PRESENT INCLUDING NEW LINK

transport, whether by default or conscious planning, is surely a speedy recipe for disaster as was proved at the time of the closure of the London Extension. In fact, the bus replacement service did not stand the test of time well.

So better rail services rather than roads is the answer, as roads needlessly disfigure the countryside and lead to pollution and often to bottlenecks at their outlets. Better rail services are the logical answer to the efficient and unobtrusive conveyance of both commuters and freight. The GC fell into all categories as it was economically designed, resourceful, modern and reliable but, alas, it is all too true that it arrived too late on the scene because human beings were reverting to putting motors on their carriages instead of horses and it is this same fact which is causing Marylebone's downfall. Let us hope that Marylebone and the name GC lives on to see its centenary.

Little Kimble *Top left*
An unusual port of call for a Saturday on the Marylebone network: an eight car class 115 DMU stops for a photographic call at this little halt north of Princes Risborough. The train was on a tour of the freight lines of Buckinghamshire and Oxfordshire as displayed by the fine headboard. Note the indicator blind which, for the benefit of the enthusiasts, had been turned round to Little Kimble instead of Excursion. Normally this train station is only used in peak hours during the week.

Princes Risborough *Top right*
A much rationalised north end of the station with the Aylesbury bay on the right of the picture and the main Banbury line disappearing off into the distance in the centre. On the left is the signal cabin and the through roads which are seldom used. Note that the points are set for a Banbury train, the 3.38pm ex Marylebone. This service is now two-hourly.

Princes Risborough
Passengers alighting at the one platform of the station from a Banbury train for the town's shops, or returning from a day out in London. Surprisingly the centre roads still remain, as does the line into the now desolate platform which bustled with activity from the local services to Thame and Oxford and Watlington, access to which was gained by the splendid footbridge which dominates the picture.

175

Marylebone

Looking northwestwards, a DMU with the 10.40am ex Aylesbury is passing the carriage washing plant before entering the small throat leading into the four platforms. Just in front of the train is the signal box, yardmaster's cabin and the oil tanks of the fuelling point. The stabled train under the water tower is seen here standing in what used to be the sidings for the old milk dock. To the left of the picture, in front of the concrete wall, a glimpse of the turntable can be seen which has proved invaluable for the series of steam workings out of Marylebone. Also worthy of note are the fine display of semaphore signals and the brick roadway just under the bridge on the right hand side.

Marylebone

An aerial view of Marylebone, taken from the top of one of the blocks of flats that now stand on the goods yard area. The outer platforms were used for express trains, while the inner set were for locals; now they only serve the Chiltern commuter belt. The rather empty looking station doubles up for a car park as can be seen here. Note the simple design of the overall canopy and the ornate lamp standards.

Marylebone

Eighty-seven years after the line opened a different kind of motive power waits to form the 1.10pm working for Aylesbury via Amersham, 15 March 1986. The terminus saw its first regular passenger service on this date in 1899 as opening celebration runs had been made six days earlier. The scene is typical of the station at midday with a few passengers boarding a waiting train. Before departure this working is coupled to another four-car unit which is 'towed' up to Aylesbury ready for rush hour traffic.